Cops Say (And Do)
The Funniest Things

GLENN MELTON

PAGE PUBLISHING, INC.
Conneaut Lake, PA

First originally published by Page Publishing 2019

ISBN 978-1-64628-253-1 (pbk)
ISBN 978-1-64628-254-8 (digital)

Printed in the United States of America

Contents

Preface

The stories you are about to read are true. The names have been changed to protect the guilty.

I spent almost thirty-five years as a law enforcement officer. At different times, I was a police officer, a juvenile probation officer, and an adult probation and parole officer. During my career, I met many people from all walks of life: cops, attorneys, judges, and probation officers, many of whom fell victim to my love of practical jokes.

Some of the stories I have recounted herein are so ridiculous you'll swear they couldn't have actually happened—but they did! Hey, this stuff is funnier than anything I could make up.

So sit back, fasten your seatbelt, and get ready for a wild ride with one of the craziest men ever to wear a badge.

Murder of the King's English

I attended college for six years, obtaining along the way a bachelor's degree in psychology and a master's degree in counseling. I was accustomed to speaking with people from educated backgrounds, and it was a real eye-opener for me to discover that not everyone uses proper grammar. Perhaps even more enlightening was the propensity of some folks to make up or totally mispronounce words, making it a challenge at times to figure out what they were trying to say.

My first experience with made-up words came when I was a juvenile probation officer. I was interviewing a male juvenile accused of having sex with an underage female. His mother was present during the interview, and in an attempt to justify the actions of her son, she said, "Well, you know, that little girl ain't really a little girl." Now, I must admit, I was confused. I thought she was implying that the object of junior's amorous attentions was a male. But she continued, "She's a little woman. You know, she's SWITCHIFIED." I had an immediate vision of this young female "switching" her posterior at this boy. I kept a straight face, but it wasn't easy. This mother seemed determined to destroy my composure, however. She admitted that her son should have used better judgment, not only in this situation but in other areas of his life as well. Clearly exasperated by his illegal behavior, she shook her head and said, "That boy been a real *disapunishment* to me."

After a year as a juvenile officer, I accepted a job as a state probation and parole officer, dealing with adult felony offenders. A large part of my duties consisted of conducting background investigations on adult offenders for circuit courts and the state parole board. During my interview with the very first person I investigated, I questioned him about his criminal history. He explained to me that he had previously been convicted of a felony, but "I took a pill." Now, having the heart of an entrepreneur, I was determined to find out what kind of pill could erase a felony conviction, as I surmised that this could be worth millions. Unfortunately, I later discovered that my client was trying to say that he had taken an APPEAL (appealed his conviction). Well, there went that dream.

One of my adult parolees worked in a pickle factory, and during one of his regularly scheduled visits to my office, he advised me that he was fatigued because he had been working a lot of overtime. It seems that the plant had received a large shipment of CREWCUMBERS.

Then there was the parolee who informed me that he had been stopped by officers of the city police department. He added, "I don't think they was regular cops. They had on them black suits. You know, like the SQUAT team." I visualized officers exiting their car and crouching, as a "squat" team might do. By now, my straight face was getting pretty good.

Eddie was what we commonly referred to as a gater, because he had been in and out of prison (through the gate) so many times. He had a girlfriend named Bertha, and periodically she would come to my office with reports of Eddie's misbehavior. I seldom acted on what she told me because I knew that within a short period of time they would be back together. On one of these occasions, Bertha informed me that she had had Eddie arrested for domestic violence and that when she went to court to testify against him, she said, "He got me so upsot that I had one o' them ATH-E-LETIC FITS." Of course, I knew what she meant, but I couldn't help having visions of her in the courtroom doing the side straddle hop.

I think the one I remember best, though, came during my interview with an elderly blind man who was applying to be pardoned from a previous conviction. In the course of gathering personal history information for my report, I inquired about his parents, both of whom, it turned out, were deceased. I asked the cause of his father's death, and without hesitation, he replied, "HEMORRHOIDS." I was thankful that this gentleman was blind, as I tried mightily but just could not suppress a smile. I was certain that he meant to say *hemorrhage,* but about a year later, I suffered from a case of hemorrhoids, and now I'm not so sure. His dad may *have* died from them—or at least wished that he could!

One thing I learned from the last encounter was never to ridicule someone; they may be able to help you later. This old fellow could never get it through his head that I was a probation officer. No, he was convinced that I was the probate judge. A couple of years later, I was in his neighborhood, a low-income public housing project, attempting to interview neighbors of a probation applicant. I wasn't having any luck getting anyone to talk to me. Just then, I saw this same old gentleman, and I called him by name. You know how you've always heard that blind people have exceptional hearing? Well, it's true. The man recognized my voice at once. He said, "Lawd, it's the probate judge. What brings you out here, Yo' Honor?" I explained my dilemma to him, and he turned immediately to his young granddaughter, who served as his guide, and said, "Chile, take me and the judge to Ms. Essie's house." When we got there, he said to the female occupant, "Essie, this here is the probate judge. You tell him what he wants to know, you understand?" I had no more difficulty obtaining the desired information. Hey, sometimes you do what works, you know?

Occasionally, I found it necessary to mispronounce or misuse words myself just to be understood. For example, any police officer who has worked the streets for more than a week will tell you that you can stand at a door all day knocking and answering the inevitable "Who is it?" with "Po-LICE," and all you will hear is "Who?" If you want someone to come to the door, you had better get used to saying, "Po-lice." Likewise, if you ask some people where they live, they will give you a blank stare. It's not that they're trying to be uncooperative, they just have no idea what you mean. Now, ask them where they *stay*, and they'll tell you where they live. Go figure.

It's not uncommon nowadays to have to interact with people who speak a language other than English. A couple of years before I retired, a Hispanic man who spoke not a word of English appeared in my office. Thankfully, he had paperwork with him that indicated that he was at the wrong place. He actually needed to be at the county probation office on the other end of the building. Now, I speak just enough Spanish to get myself in trouble, so I said, "Senor Gonzalez, venga aqui, por favor" (come here, please). He dutifully followed me to the county probation office, where I told the secretary, "Este es Senor Gonzalez, and he no habla ingles (he does not speak English). Buena suerte" (good luck). As I started for the door, the panicky secretary yelled, "You get back here and help me!" I turned and said with a smile, "No, no, senorita, usted no entiende. No es mi problemo. Es *su* problemo" (You don't understand. This is not my problem, it's your problem).

Then you have people who can't understand or speak the language—until they have to. I once had a parolee named Lamar Lassiter. Lamar was a grave digger by trade, as were most of his brothers. Grave digging is a lot like house painting: there are times when you have no work, and you can utilize these periods to get drunk. Lamar's wife, Cindy, called me one day to advise that Lamar had gone on a bender and was staying at a small motel out in the county. I don't know if this is a nationwide trend, but in the southeast, many of the mom-and-pop motels have been bought by foreigners who generally live on the premises. Such was the case with this one. I went to the office and encountered the owner. I tried to tell him who I was and who I was looking for; however, he seemed to be having a great deal of difficulty understanding me. "Who? Las…Lassiter…uh…"

Finally I perceived that I was being screwed with, so I reached into my suit coat pocket and produced my departmental identification, a large, shiny gold badge, which I slapped down on the counter in front of Mr. "I-No-Speaka-de-English." I said, "Look, here's the deal: I'm going to start over there at room number one and knock on every door until I find Mr. Lassiter. When the occupants answer the door, I'm going to identify myself with this badge. That won't cause you any problems, right?" I knew better because this seedy dump was known as a flophouse for drunks, druggies, and prostitutes. Suddenly, a light went on, and the owner "understood" much better. He said, "He in room thirteen." And he was! Along with his brother, Landon Lassiter. (After the birth of their first child, Gene, Lamar's parents had fallen in love with the literary device called alliteration; all of their subsequent children had first names beginning with the letter *L*.) Landon was about six eight, but he was as wasted as Lamar, so he didn't give me any trouble as I arrested Lamar. They had spent several days consuming vast quantities of a popular cheap wine, empty half-gallon bottles of which they had placed all around the room in some bizarre decorating scheme (early alcoholic? I don't know).

As a police officer working in a town bordered by a military base, I frequently encountered people who spoke little or no English. Communication with them was difficult at best and sometimes required inventive solutions, like hand signals and even pantomime. One night I was dispatched to a neighborhood in reference to a person behaving strangely. Upon my arrival, I quickly ascertained that the offender was drunk as a skunk (actually, I don't recall ever seeing a drunk skunk). He was an oriental, small in stature, maybe five six. It was clear that I was going to have to take him into custody, but when I attempted to lay hands on him, he pulled away from my grasp and backed off a few paces. Apparently he had been watching too many ninja movies—or maybe he was really a black belt, I don't know. At any rate, he went into a martial arts crouch, threw his hands up, and said, "Ooh, KARATE." It had been a long night, and I just wasn't in the mood for games. So I pulled out my .357 revolver, a huge, intimidating weapon, pointed it at him, and said, "Smith and Wesson." I guess the language of the gun is universal, because he suddenly stood erect, shot his hands straight up, and very quietly said, "You win."

Then there were occasions when a person I was interviewing used perfect grammar, but what they said caught me completely off guard. Like the time I was assigned to complete a presentence investigation on Freddie Ben Allen, who had entered a plea of guilty to one count of second-degree murder. Allen had shot his wife, Mary, with a shotgun in their home. He claimed that the shooting was accidental. What made the case so interesting was that Mary Allen was a secretary employed by US Congressman Bob Baxter. She and Congressman Baxter's assistant, Wilmer Vandenburg, worked in the congressman's local office.

This was a sensational case that had engendered a great deal of publicity, so I was intent on producing the best report of my life.

Accordingly, I left no stone unturned, interviewing everybody I could find who had ever known the perpetrator and/or the victim. These included doctors, attorneys, college professors, and ministers. It occurred to me that Congressman Baxter should be allowed some input, so I called his local office. Mr. Vandenburg informed me that the congressman was, at that moment, on the floor of Congress, but he said, "I know he'll want to talk to you. Hold while I get him on the phone." Apparently they had some type of telephone patching system because in just a minute or so, I was speaking with the congressman himself.

Now, this was only the second time in my life that I had talked with a congressman, so I tried to sound very professional. I told Congressman Baxter why I had called, then I said, "Congressman, I know that you know Mr. Allen personally and have for several years. Inasmuch as he killed your secretary, I know that it would be difficult, but do you think you could give me a relatively unbiased opinion of his character?" Congressman Baxter was very folksy, and he was a politician through and through. He spoke to me like he had known me all his life. He said, "Why, sure, Glenn, I'll be glad to give you a totally unbiased, objective opinion. Frankly, I think Freddie Ben Allen is a rotten, no-good sonofabitch!" After I regained my composure, I thanked the congressman for his time. And I quoted his comments verbatim in my report.

There were times when a person didn't have to open his mouth to test the limits of my self-control. Take the case of Ronald Parsons.

During a term of court, it is not unusual for a probation and parole officer to be assigned several persons whom a judge has just placed on a period of supervised probation. I am organized to the point of frequently being called anal-retentive, and I would set aside one day to meet individually with these new probationers for the purpose of explaining to them the conditions of their probation. It was not uncommon for me to instruct five or six of these people, one at a time, during such a day, and I sincerely believe that after several hours of repeating the same rules over and over, I could have done this in my sleep. On one such day, I had just finished with one new client when our senior secretary, Wanda Taylor, advised me via the intercom that I had another waiting. I told her to send him back to my office. I retrieved his file and got ready to meet with him, but frankly, nothing could have prepared me for what happened next.

Ronald Parsons was a typical young offender who had entered a plea of guilty to a minor felony charge and been granted probation in lieu of being sent to the penitentiary. By reading his file, I learned that Ronald was about five eight and weighed one fifty. Still, when he turned the corner into my office, I know that my chin had to have hit my desk.

First of all, he looked like a hand grenade had exploded in his face. He had piercings everywhere you can imagine and in some places you probably can't. In addition, his medium-length hair was spiked—and dyed blue! Yes, I said blue. Still, I didn't crack a smile. Believe me, it wasn't easy. Ronald was reasonably intelligent and very polite, so the interview went well, in spite of his bizarre appearance. Right up until the last, that is. See, people on probation or parole are required to either work or attend school. When I explained this requirement to Ronald, he said, quite seriously, "I've been having a hard time finding a job." My stoicism was almost destroyed by that one; still I took a couple of deep breaths and replied, as sincerely as possible, "You don't say."

Wanda Taylor, the secretary who had sent Ronald back to see me without a heads-up, was a long-time friend of mine. I could not believe that she had set me up like that (well, yes, I could). I waited a few minutes, as I knew she would expect me to come out of my office right away to get her back. Then I casually strolled into the secretarial area as though I didn't have a care in the world. I said, "Boy, it's been a busy day." I cast a sideways glance at Wanda and was pretty sure I could see a tear forming in her eye. She was containing her glee, but just barely. I eased up close to her desk, then I made a swift move, placing my mouth right beside her ear, and said, "You ever set me up like that again—" Before I could finish my sentence, Wanda let out what can best be described as a howl. She was joined in her cacophonous revelry by the other secretaries, who, of course, were in on the gag. I continued, "You EVER do that to me again—"

Howwlll...

"And I swear, I'll kill you. And that's not a threat, it's a promise."

From that day forward, all the secretaries referred to Ronald as parrot head.

Buddy Calhoun was as dumb as a rock. Yes, that is an insult—to the rock. He was married to a woman named Shelley, who was an on-again, off-again (pardon the pun) prostitute. Buddy was not fond of work, so in order to pay the rent and put food on the table, Shelly would occasionally go out and ply her trade. Buddy did not like for her to do this, so they stayed at each other's throat much of the time.

One day Shelly called me to inform me that Buddy was physically unable to come to my office for his regular monthly report. It seems that just the night before, in her words, "Buddy sat down on a pair of scissors, and they cut an artery in his leg. He almost bled to death." I told Shelly that as soon as Buddy was ambulatory, I would expect to see him. Then I got to thinking. He sat on a pair of scissors? And they just happened to be turned point up? Sounded pretty fishy, so I called the patrol division of the local police department, and guess what? Officers had answered a call to Buddy and Shelly's residence the previous evening. Seems they had been arguing when Shelly grabbed a pair of scissors and started chasing Buddy up the stairs, stabbing at him. One of her thrusts found its mark in his leg, and he continued running, resulting in his leg being laid open like a fish's belly.

About a week later, Shelly and Buddy—on crutches—sauntered into my office wrapped around each other like kudzu on a telephone pole. I advised them that I knew what had really happened and asked if they planned to stay together (hey, you think I'd go to sleep in the same house with a woman who had tried to kill me? Not!). So Buddy got these big cow eyes and said, "Oh, yeah, we're gonna stay together, 'cause she LOVES me." I replied, "Damn good thing she doesn't hate you." Went right over their heads. I think. But then, I really didn't care.

Strange Encounters of
the Bizarre Kind

During my thirty-four years as a law enforcement officer, I have encountered several—what's a politically correct way to phrase this—*different* people. *Very* different. The bad part of it is, often you have no warning that they are disturbed until you are engaged in contact with them. Sometimes this presents a real danger to the officer, and other times it's just funny as hell. Take my encounter with probationer Tim Johnson's mother.

It was a beautiful sunny day, and I had taken the opportunity to leave my office and make some required visits to homes of my probationers and parolees, to whom we euphemistically referred as clients. Tim Johnson lived with his mother on a busy street in a lower income neighborhood. I had made several visits to the home, each time speaking with his mother and never having had any reason to suspect anything unusual. On this day, however, things would turn out to be anything *but* usual.

As soon as I knocked on the front door, I heard a female voice asking, "Who is it?" Now, this was not an uncommon occurrence; however, when she opened the door, Mrs. Johnson stuck just her head out and said, "I can't talk in here. My house is bugged." At this point, I still was not concerned. I thought she meant that Tim was home and that she wanted to tell me something that she did not want him to hear. As soon as she walked out onto the porch though, things changed. Dramatically. She began making statements clearly identifying her as suffering from paranoid schizophrenia, a serious mental illness, such as "The man next door has my house bugged" and "There's four brown houses on this block. Don't you see? Quadruplicate!" Then she grabbed my arm, pointed excitedly to a woman across the street who was shaking out her doormat, and declared, "Look! She's giving them a signal." Finally finding my voice, I said, "Who?" She replied, "I don't know, but she's giving them a signal!"

Having ascertained that I might stay healthier if I left the scene posthaste, I was edging toward my car, with Mrs. Johnson holding onto my arm with a death grip. I got to my vehicle, opened the door, and said, "I'll see you later," whereupon Mrs. Johnson eyed me suspiciously and replied, "That's what they *all* say." Well, by now I had regained my composure, and this little scenario was just too good to let pass without a little tweaking. I pried Mrs. Johnson loose from my arm and said, "Maybe I need to go check this lady out and see just what she is up to." Mrs. Johnson looked at me earnestly and said, "Would you?"

So I walked across the street and introduced myself to this elderly lady. I told her about my client, Tim, across the street and told her to advise me if he caused her any trouble. Then I walked back over to Mrs. Johnson and said, "Well, you were right. She was giving them a signal." "Who?" she asked. I replied, "Well she wouldn't say, but it's somebody here in the neighborhood. She's a CIA agent, and they're conducting an investigation into an international spy ring. That's all she could say. Now please don't tell anybody. That might blow her cover." As her eyes bugged out and her mouth fell open, I bade Mrs. Johnson farewell and departed.

Mrs. Johnson's daughter also worked for the state, and I happened to know her, so when I got back to my office, I called her at work. I said, "Dana, does the term 'paranoid schizophrenia' mean anything to you?" To which she replied, "Oh yes, that's what they said Mama had the last time she was at the state mental hospital." I was still a little shaken, and I said, "The LAST TIME? Do you think JUST MAYBE I should have been privy to this information?" Dana apologized and said, "I guess we're going to have to take her back to the hospital. She just called me with some wild story about spies and the CIA."

It's funny in retrospect, but encounters with mentally unbalanced people can turn deadly in an instant.

Witness the case of Mark James. During my first meeting with Mark, I knew something was wrong, and I knew what it was. It might have been the photographs he brought with him, one of which showed an oak tree that was probably fifty years old. Mark informed me that he had attended a party in the home of a friend and that when he entered the house, the tree was not there. I just couldn't pass up the opportunity to inject a little levity, so I said, "Must have been one long party." No, he told me, the tree had been brought and placed there by a police officer, who was hiding behind it when Mark left the house. I thought, man, if that officer can pick up a mature oak tree, I'd sure like to have him with me on my next arrest.

Not only did Mark suffer from delusions of persecution, he also had delusions of grandeur, common with paranoid schizophrenics. He informed me that he could remove the nervous system from a cat. Again, I just couldn't resist a little humorous verbal sparring, so I said, "Well, I can too, Mark, but it would sure ruin the cat's day." Mark didn't like me very much. I never could understand why.

I mentioned earlier that encounters with mentally disturbed people can be challenging and often downright dangerous, and Mark is a case in point. He was not abiding by the conditions of his probation, so I wrote a report detailing his violations, and the probationary judge declared him delinquent and ordered him arrested. Following standard procedure, I took another probation officer with me, and we drove to the trailer park where Mark lived with his parents. When we parked the car, Mark was standing outside his trailer. It was obvious that he knew why we were there, as he began running toward his front door. This is where it gets hairy.

I knew from talking with him that Mark's father kept a loaded shotgun in his bedroom. I had no doubt that Mark was heading for that gun and that if he laid his hands on it, either he would shoot us or we would be forced to shoot him. As he entered the bedroom where the shotgun was kept, I was just a step behind him, and I could see the gun propped up in a corner beside the bed's headboard. Fortunately, the furniture was arranged in such a way that Mark had to run around the foot of the bed to get to the gun. Recognizing this, I made a leap worthy of Superman across the center of the bed, tackled Mark, and slammed him through the trailer's thin interior paneling before he could reach the shotgun. By then, the other officer had arrived, and we subdued Mark and handcuffed him. Whew! Close.

Sometimes reasonably normal people may experience what is known as a psychotic episode, where they lose total touch with reality. This type of disorder is usually temporary and may be the result of drug use, lack of sleep, or rarely, total immersion for an extended time in some fantasy activity, such as a computer game. Even though they generally recover from this psychosis, they can be dangerous to law enforcement personnel while they are in la-la land.

I encountered such a man about three o'clock one morning. I was dispatched to investigate a possible prowler in a trailer park. I almost immediately located the suspect, who informed me that I should not, um, *futz* with him, as he was the dungeon master from the popular (at that time) game Dungeons and Dragons. It quickly became obvious that rational discussion with this guy was not going to be possible, as he was totally whacked (that's a professional psychological term). I attempted to take him into protective custody and discovered that he really did not have being arrested on his agenda. After a prolonged wrestling match, I was able to subdue him; however, by then I was too exhausted to handcuff him, so I just shoved him into the back of my patrol car while I regained my stamina.

Well, the dungeon master was not happy about being bested, so he grabbed the mesh screen that separated him from me and began pulling on it and *growling* (I am not making this up). I was standing outside the car with the passenger front door open, and I said, "Get your hands off my screen." His response was to pull harder and growl louder. I warned him once more: "GET…YOUR…HANDS… OFF…MY…SCREEN." Same response. I took out my night stick and slammed it against the front of the screen, striking all ten of his fingers. He jerked his hands back and made a sound roughly akin to "AROOO!" I heard no more from him all the way to the jail.

Not all mentally disturbed people are dangerous. Sometimes they can be pretty nice. You just have to realize that they are in their own world and that their perceptions may seriously diverge from reality. If you can accept that you are not going to change them and just go with the flow, the encounter can be safe and even pleasant.

Like the time I was sent on a "meet a party" (nature of problem not specified) call. The address was in a low-income section of town, but the small house was neat and well-kept. As I approached the front door, an elderly gentleman seated on the porch greeted me with "You just need to take that crazy old bitch to jail." This sort of raised my apprehension level, but as I entered the home's only bedroom, I found a sweet elderly female, very neatly groomed, sitting in bed wearing a satin bed jacket. She spoke very rationally and first apologized for "bothering" me. I assured her that her call was no bother, that I was there to help her. She then pointed to a photograph hanging over her bed and said, "That's a picture of my mother. There are demons hiding behind it, and they told me that they are coming out at three o'clock this afternoon to kill me." I checked my watch. It was ten minutes until three. So I said to her, "Well, we'll see about that." I made a show of unsnapping my pistol holster and being sure that my gun was loose and ready for action. Then I sat down in a chair beside her bed, and we began to talk. She told me all about her life, which consumed about twenty minutes. At ten past three, I pointed out the time to her, and she said, "Why, those demons lied to me. I won't believe another thing they say." I bade her farewell, and as far as I know, we were never dispatched to that address again. Not all schizophrenics are so easily dissuaded from their paranoid delusions, and I often wondered whether this poor old woman was faking just to have somebody to talk to.

A common misconception is that the only way to approach a mentally ill person is with force. Actually, although they may have a serious psychological disorder, many of them are at least average in intelligence, and they know when they are being talked down to or bullied. One night my rookie and I were dispatched to a residence to serve a warrant on a man who had allegedly assaulted his sister. As we parked in front of the house, we were approached by the subject's brother, who advised, "You're gonna have to fight him. Happens every time the cops come after him." So I told my rookie, "Bring your nightstick, but put it on your belt. Don't draw it unless we really have to fight this guy." I never held my nightstick in my hand unless I anticipated using it or unless I was trying to create an atmosphere of serious intimidation in order to avoid a fight.

We then followed the brother into his house, where we met Clarence, a large physically imposing man. Like I said, my experience has been that your approach may set the tone for the whole encounter, so I extended my hand to Clarence, introducing myself and my partner. Then I said, "Can we all sit down for a second?" Clarence dutifully complied, and my rookie and I took seats on either side of him. I continued, "Clarence, look, I wasn't here, and I have no idea what happened. But your sister has sworn out a warrant on you, so I need to take you to jail. Okay?" Clarence's next move scared the crap out of me.

He jumped to his feet, but instead of becoming combative as his brother had warned, he turned around and placed his hands behind his back for me to apply handcuffs. This was followed by an uneventful trip to jail, where he cooperated fully and politely with the staff. Would this approach work every time? Probably not, but it never hurts to try. The force continuum can always be escalated if required, but when you start at or near the top, you don't have much place to go.

Occasionally you run into a person whose behavior is indicative of mental illness, but actually the problem turns out to be something completely different. About two o'clock on a humid summer morning, I was pulling into a fast-food restaurant to get some breakfast. I had my window rolled down so that I could hear any unusual activity, like a burglary in progress or a fight. Suddenly, this wiry woman wearing a wild expression on her face came running up to my open window and began waving her hands frantically and grunting. My first impression was that she was crazy, but about the time I decided that, she made a writing motion, indicating her need for pencil and paper. Of course, then I realized that she was a deaf mute.

She wrote that she and her boyfriend were having a domestic disturbance, so I put her in my car, called for a backup unit (domestics are by far the most dangerous situations police officers face), and proceeded to her address. Well, lo and behold, upon our arrival, we discover that the boyfriend is also a deaf mute. So here the two of them are signing vigorously at each other and grunting. I looked at my fellow officer and asked, "Do you understand any of this?" He replied, "Not a word." About that time, the woman looked at her boyfriend and flipped him off, and he returned the gesture. I smiled at the other officer and said, "I must be getting the hang of this sign language, 'cause I sure understood that."

Beyond a shadow of a doubt, however, the funniest encounter I ever had with a deranged person occurred about three o'clock one morning, when I was dispatched to a report of a domestic disturbance. Upon my arrival, I found a middle-aged female standing in the street. This was not the first time I had encountered this. Sometimes, when two parties are having a dispute, one of them wants to be sure and have the opportunity to present his or her side first, so they will "greet" you as you arrive at the scene. Well, this lady's first statement to me was "Officer, I want you to get these people out of my house."

Now, I learned a long time ago that unless someone's life or health is in imminent danger, it's best to get all the facts before rushing headlong into a situation. It can keep you from making a mistake, and it may even keep you alive. So before I "threw these people out of her house," I first wanted to know if she owned the house. She assured me that she did. I then asked if the person she wanted removed was her husband. The only way you can "put out" a bona fide resident of a house is if you are taking that person to jail. She replied that there were several people and that she did not know them. Suddenly, I'm on high alert, thinking that we have a burglary in progress. I reached for my radio microphone to call for backup, but a little voice in my head (you have one of those, don't you?) told me to ask another question, so I said, "Where in the house are these people located?" To which she replied, "I don't know, but you won't be able to see them anyway."

By now I was pretty sure I had a loon on my hands, so I said, "Why not?" And she said, "They can take on different forms." I nodded understandingly and asked her, "Do you know where these people are from?" She answered with a firm "Mars!" I nodded again and said, "I thought so. We've been having lots of trouble out of those guys. I'm going in the house and get rid of them. They're extremely dangerous, so whatever you hear, don't come in."

Another patrol unit had been dispatched to assist, which, as I mentioned earlier, was common practice when responding to a report of a domestic disturbance. Now that I had a clear understanding of the situation, I knew his presence would not be required, so I advised him via radio to disregard.

I went into the house, located the kitchen, and pulled out some pots and pans, which I commenced to beat on the kitchen counter while simultaneously shouting at the "martians" to leave. I actually considered firing a round through the ceiling, but I would have had to write a report explaining why I did that, and somehow I did not think that "shooting at martians" would be conducive to career advancement. When I was through, I pulled my tie down, mussed up my hair, and "staggered" out of the house and back to the complainant. I told her, "Well, it was one heck of a fight, but I got rid of them. I don't think you'll be bothered anymore." She thanked me profusely, and as far as I know, she never called back. Of course, I often wondered if it was because she actually believed me or if she thought I was crazier than she was.

After a call, procedure was for the officer to notify dispatch by radio that he was back in service and what, if any, action he had taken. The call might sound like, "107 [unit number], 10-8 [available], report" or "107, 10-8, arrest." I guess when I said, "107, 10-8, ran some martians off," the dispatcher must have thought I was in trouble and trying to let her know because after a long pause, she said, "Are you 10-4 [okay]?" I replied, "I'm fine, but this woman you sent me to see is nutty as a fruitcake."

He Didn't Really Say
That—Did He?

And speaking of radio traffic (nice segue, don't you think?), modern-day police officers have a device in the trunk of their vehicles that they refer to—not fondly—as a sergeant in the trunk. What it does is keep tabs for the dispatcher on the movement of, and radio traffic from, that particular vehicle. It's actually a great safety device. Say a dispatcher can't raise a unit on the radio or the officer advises that he is chasing somebody on foot. The dispatcher knows exactly where the vehicle is so that backup can be sent. It would also be very helpful during a vehicle pursuit, as the dispatcher could announce the officer's location and direction of travel, allowing that officer to keep his attention focused on the pursuit without having to read and radio street names. Unfortunately for the officer, however, this device has a downside as well. If he decides to sit at one location for a long period of time or if he ventures off his assigned beat, the evidence is clear. Also, he is not able to make any radio transmission without being identified. Of course, a professional officer would never do such a thing anyway. Would he? Well…

When I was a police officer, these nefarious machines had not been invented. Or if they had, we did not have them. This meant that if an officer using the radio chose not to identify himself, there was no way to determine who was broadcasting. Accordingly, it was not uncommon to hear snatches of popular songs. Sometimes, especially late at night when things were deathly quiet, the radio would transmit a healthy belch…or worse.

Early one morning, the city had quieted down, and we were all fighting sleep. It was a very foggy morning, with visibility limited to just a few feet. Suddenly, over the radio came a slow, deep voice that declared, "Sure is foggy out here." I got so tickled I had to pull my car over. In about a minute, Mr. Weatherman repeated his forecast: "Sure is foggy out here." The watch commander was a captain, and he had heard enough. He got on the radio and demanded, "Unit calling, identify yourself!" There was a lengthy pause, followed by Officer Anonymous, who replied, "Ain't *that* foggy out here." There was much speculation as to the officer's identity, but as far as I know, no one ever found out who it was.

During the heat of the moment—a fight or maybe a foot pursuit—an officer's adrenaline starts flowing, and radio traffic can sometimes be less than professional. One of our sergeants got into a struggle with an offender and was unable to subdue him. His call for backup was "Send me another unit! This guy's being an asshole."

One day I had just come on duty and was sitting at an intersection during a particularly violent thunderstorm. I have had the experience of almost being struck by lightning on three separate occasions, so I am not especially fond of it. Suddenly, with a tremendous bang, lightning struck a power line that crossed the road directly in front of me. A huge fireball rolled down the line and into a residential neighborhood. Knowing that such strikes can cause house fires, I attempted to explain the situation to my dispatcher and advise that I would be in the neighborhood looking for damage. Apparently, the strike had caused some kind of electrical problem with my radio; the dispatcher kept responding to my transmission with "10-9?" (repeat your traffic). Nerves still taut from the lightning strike, I finally snapped and said, "LISTEN, DAMMIT!" Unfortunately, they heard that one. Apparently no supervisor did, as I was never counseled about radio etiquette.

The city where I worked as a police officer had within its borders a number of trailer parks. Early one peaceful morning, maybe four o'clock, I was dispatched to an address in one of them. The radio code given to me was for a parking complaint. Parking complaint? At four in the morning? Oh well, I figured maybe somebody had come out to go to work and found his driveway blocked. Thankfully, as I entered the trailer court, a man ran up to my car and identified himself as the complainant. What he told me had nothing to do with parking. It seems that he had seen a vehicle occupied by two men parked by a trailer whose owner he knew to be away from home. He suspected—correctly, I'm sure—that their intent was to burglarize the house. I immediately notified dispatch by radio of the true nature of the call, then I turned off my headlights and eased up to the address.

Sure enough, there was the occupied vehicle. Upon seeing me, the driver began an oh-so-slow exit from the trailer park. I was directly behind him, calling in his license plate number to dispatch. As soon as the vehicle reached the main road, I made a serious tactical blunder. I activated my blue lights.

Well, of course, the driver kicked in the afterburner, and the chase was on. A few seconds later, the dispatcher drawled, in a sleepy voice, "One oh seven [my unit number], that tag comes back stolen." I looked at my speedometer, and we were already up to eighty and climbing. I guess the tension of the moment just had to come out, so I replied, "No SHIT! Well, I'm in hot pursuit of that stolen tag." Long story short: the bad guys got about a block lead on me, bailed out, and fled on foot. We didn't catch them, but we did recover a stolen vehicle. The supervisors must have been at the doughnut shop because I never caught flak about that response either.

Occasionally, officers are dispatched on calls that are so unusual that no radio check-in code can fully explain what they actually did. Case in point: our city had an ordinance which forbade keeping farm-type animals within the city limits. Nevertheless, we had an elderly gentleman living in a poor section near downtown who kept a mule in his backyard. This situation was tolerated because from time to time, he would hitch old Dobbin to his wagon and give the neighborhood kids rides, which they loved.

Now, old Dobbin was pretty well-behaved, but sometimes he would start feeling his wild oats and escape from his fenced yard. Each time this happened, we were called to round him up, which normally required several of us, as the mule was wily and hard to corral. After one such episode, one of my fellow officers called in on the radio, "All units 10-8 [back in service], one mule roped." The not-unexpected response was a chorus of unidentified officers braying like jackasses.

We had a female lieutenant who was very conscious of officer and departmental liability. If one of us got into a vehicle pursuit, she would radio us and ask our speed and the reason for the chase. If the speed was not to her liking or if she did not think a pursuit was justified by the circumstances, she would order it terminated. This, of course, did not sit well with us. There is not too much worse in police work than having to break off a pursuit and watching the offender thumb his nose at you or give you a one-finger salute.

I got behind a very fast vehicle one night and notified dispatch of the situation. I was immediately radioed by this lieutenant, who requested my speed and the reason for the pursuit. I picked up my radio microphone, put it directly against my lips, and said, "Scrrggg, bzzzt fahhh, nwagm naar," feigning unintelligible transmission. The lieutenant tried a couple more times, and I responded the same way. She finally gave up, and I was able to catch the offender. At the end of my shift, the lieutenant said, "Melton, what was wrong with your radio? I couldn't understand a word you said." I replied, "Well, Lieutenant, I think the problem was that I was going so fast that my antenna was bending over and making contact with my trunk lid, causing a short." She turned sort of pale and said, "Oh my god! How fast were you going?" I said, "Well, I stopped looking at 120. I figured I needed to keep my eyes on the road." As far as I know, she never figured out that I was lying.

Of course, a radio can suffer a legitimate malfunction. It was not uncommon for the transmit button on some officer's radio microphone to get stuck in the "on" position, after which all of us could hear everything he or she said. Sometimes we were privy to some really juicy tidbits of conversation. I never had my radio microphone stick, but I did have a stuck mike on my public address system one day. This meant that every word said in my vehicle was broadcast to the outside. I was a training officer at the time, so I had a rookie riding with me. We were driving slowly down a main thoroughfare and exchanging comments about various pedestrians we saw.

Unfortunately, our observations were being heard by the very people we were talking about, and some of our language was, ahem, a little crude. After a couple of blocks of receiving some rather hostile stares, I began to suspect that we had a problem. We determined that the mike was stuck in the open position, and the only way to disable it was to turn off the siren, as the PA system and siren were on the same circuit. After that, I made it a point to check my PA system before saying something I didn't want the whole world to hear.

As mentioned in another chapter, our radio protocol called for the initiating unit to identify itself, then the responding unit would reply in the same way. For example, a typical transmission might go: "Headquarters to 109." The paged officer would then respond, "109." When we worked first watch, which began at midnight, it was not uncommon to get sleepy, especially after about two o'clock, when the city had pretty much settled down. The body has an internal mechanism that thinks that by a certain time, you need to be in bed, no matter how much sleep you may have had during the day. Most of us had hidey holes on our beats where we could sneak off to for a few winks. As some of our officers had discovered the hard way, trying to fight the drowsies can cause you to doze off while driving. Not good.

My sleepy time was just before dawn. I would hide in my hole and try to just barely nod, not getting so deep into sleep that I wouldn't hear the radio if I were called. Apparently, one morning I drifted too far off. I awoke to the dispatcher shouting, "ONE…OH… TWO!" Now, as I said, my response should have been "102." But I was still half asleep, and besides, the tone of her voice had really pissed me off. So I answered, "WHAT?" I did hear about that one.

One night, I was on evening watch (3-11). It wasn't very late, maybe nine o'clock, but I had been working several part-time jobs to make ends meet, and I was really tired. I had another unit meet me at a manufacturing concern, which was way off the road where I knew we would not be seen. We pulled up window to window, and I said, "I need to catch a few winks. If you'll listen for the radio, I'll swap out in about thirty minutes and let you nap." Sounded like a plan to him, so I slouched down in my seat and proceeded to dreamland. I awoke to this sound: *Bam-bam-bam-bam-bam-bam*! I looked over at my buddy, and if my eyes were as wide as his, it's a wonder they didn't pop out of my head. That night was when I learned what the Bible means by speaking in tongues. I looked at him and said, "OOBAHGUKLADAMUH?" To which he replied, "ARGHHUMADAGWOOP!" Now, maybe you can't decipher all that technical jargon, but we knew *exactly* what we were saying: SOMEBODY'S SHOOTING AT US! LET'S GET THE HELL OUT OF HERE! No, we had no intention of fleeing, but neither did we intend to stay in one spot like a couple of sitting ducks.

We knew about where the shooter was from hearing the gunfire, so we cranked our cars, planning to circle him. Meanwhile, my fellow officer gets on the radio to report our situation and call for backup. Only problem is, he was still speaking in tongues: "RABAGAARFOOFAMOTS!" Dispatch couldn't understand him, so they said, "10-9?" (repeat). Finally I got on the radio before he could and very calmly said, "SHUT UP, JACK. Headquarters, 307 and 327 are at Quality Pre-Cast Concrete on George Washington Boulevard. We've just had six shots fired at us, request immediate backup."

Well, the story has a good ending. I caught the shooter coming out of the woods and persuaded him to surrender his weapon (pretty easy decision when you're out of ammo and looking down the barrel of a .357 magnum in the hands of a very pissed-off cop). Several days later, I ran into the dispatcher who was on duty that night. He said, "Man, you sounded like you were ordering take-out for dinner. Were you really that calm?" I replied, "Well, let's put it this way. I doubt if you could have driven a straight pin up my butt with a sledge hammer, but I knew if I couldn't tell you guys where we were, you couldn't send the cavalry."

See, I've never allowed myself to be consumed by fear. Now that probably sounds boastful, and I don't mean it that way at all. In fact, I will tell you emphatically that I have had times when my apprehension level was off the scale. Sort of like the guy who said that he and his wife had never had an argument, but they *had* had moments of intense fellowship. And I may actually be indulging, unintentionally, in a semantic exercise. Let's face it: if you get in a life-threatening situation and don't have a healthy amount of apprehension, you just aren't real bright. But to me, at least, apprehension is what makes you cautious and leads to good decisions. What I call fear, on the other hand, is a paralyzing emotion that makes one unable to think, talk, or act effectively. Apprehension can keep you alive, but sooner or later, fear will get you killed. Your lesson for the day is now complete. You may return to your previous activity.

From the Department of Odd Coincidences: Many months after I penned (or whatever you call writing on a computer) my admittedly unscientific opinion about the difference between fear and apprehension, I chanced upon an article in a national magazine that lent some credibility to my theory. According to a science writer, the area of the human brain that perceives danger is the amygdala. When it tells the brain's prefrontal cortex that a highly dangerous situation has been encountered, thinking clearly becomes difficult, sometimes causing one to become paralyzed by fear. In some of us though (probably all fools like me), that doesn't happen. In fact, we may even be energized by the situation and the often instant decisions it calls for.

The writer points out that having a good grasp of how to handle the problem often comes from training. He gave another example, but I immediately thought of the airline captain whose jet engines were totally disabled by a bird strike. He had an airplane full of passengers for whose safety he was responsible. What he did not have was enough altitude to reach any airport. Instead of panicking, he carefully and methodically landed this huge unwieldy beast with zero power in the river. Was he apprehensive? Oh, you can bet your booty on that. But he did not allow fear to destroy his capacity for planning and action.

Here's another story that involves staying calm in the face of serious danger. And this one I can speak to personally because I was involved. Four months after I retired, I was driving my pickup truck on an errand. Any trip from my home requires travel on the highway off which I live. I had reached the posted speed limit off 55 and was on a stretch of road with double yellow lines, which, in my state, is meant to signal no passing either way. I distinctly remember my first thought at what happened next was "You have got to be kidding."

Less than fifty yards in front of me and traveling in the opposite direction, a young man had, for reasons known only to him, decided to pass the vehicle he was following. He was so close when he began his maneuver that I could see his skin tone. I remember thinking that he was Hispanic. Not that that has any significance; I say it only to indicate how close we were to each other.

It always amazes me how fast one's mind can assess a situation and formulate a plan to handle it. Probably no more than two seconds elapsed from the time I saw this kid start to pass until the instant of impact. In that brief window, I determined that a collision was inevitable. If we had met head-on, our combined speed at impact would have been approximately one hundred miles per hour. Having worked wrecks like that, I knew that neither of us would survive a crash at that speed. I looked at my only escape route, which was the right shoulder of the road. I had maybe eighteen inches of usable shoulder, after which I would have dropped into a five-foot-deep ditch, at the end of which was a dirt berm topped by a concrete residential driveway. I would have impacted that berm either upside down or on my side at probably forty miles per hour; not a good alternative. I got as far over as possible without entering the ditch, at which point the other driver struck my truck on the driver's door, continuing down the side of the vehicle and sending me into a counter-clockwise spin on the roadway.

Now, wild child that I was in my feckless youth, I had practiced putting my car into slides on dirt roads and wet paved streets, so I knew the proper way to recover from a slide: turn the steering wheel in the direction of the skid and apply a judicious amount of throttle. This time, it wouldn't work. Only after my mangled truck had come to rest on the opposite side of the highway, after spinning 270 degrees, did I understand the reason. The impact had knocked my left rear wheel completely off the axle, which had also been pulled loose, causing the driveshaft to drop. Getting the picture? I had no power going to my one good drive wheel.

The most amazing thing about the whole accident was that, although my truck and his were destroyed, neither of us sustained a scratch. Still broke my heart though, because my beloved truck, which had every conceivable option, was five years old and had only sixteen thousand miles on the odometer. The other driver's first words to me were "I didn't see you." Okay, let's see: a full-size blood-red truck, with the headlights burning, and he didn't see me? Can you say texting? I knew you could. The whole point of this lengthy story, though, is to point out that I kept my wits about me and planned— albeit in a big-ass hurry—a course of action that just possibly saved two lives. I remember when I had spun ninety degrees and was still making some speed. I realized that my truck was pointed at some large trees just off the road. I expected to hit these head-on, and I recall thinking, "I'm going to get hurt real bad." But there was no fear. It was like, "I think I'll have a sandwich for lunch." No attempt at macho bravado here, just an observation that some people can handle crises, and some can't. And I have no idea why.

I worked for a year as a juvenile probation officer in the very early seventies. This was before I was married (for the first time), and I used to spend some evenings with the youth services detectives of the local police department. One night, I was riding with Jackie Valeria. Jackie was a native New Yorker, and he still had the accent. He wasn't very large; however, he was a trained and experienced amateur boxer, and he wasn't afraid of the devil himself.

It was a quiet summer evening, and police cars in those days had no air conditioning, so the windows of the unmarked car were down. Suddenly, the police radio began broadcasting a lookout for a vehicle wanted in connection with a possible kidnapping. Seems a witness had observed a man in a nearby housing project beating a woman and forcing her into his car. We were nearby, so we scoured the area, without success. We were on the way back downtown to police headquarters when I spotted the suspect vehicle directly in front of us.

Relying on his years of experience, Jackie did not rush headlong into the situation. Instead, he radioed our position so that other units could converge on the location of the planned vehicle stop, in case there was any violence or the driver decided to flee. As soon as he was satisfied that other units were close enough, Jackie attempted to activate our car's siren. No luck. Also in the police vehicle was a handheld spotlight with a blue lens cover. I grabbed this and aimed it at the driver's window. And that damn thing didn't work either.

A clearly exasperated Jackie yelled at me, "Dammit, he's on your side of the car. Do something!" I had absolutely no clue what to do, but I stuck my head out the car's passenger window and yelled "Woo woo woo" in my best imitation of a siren. This was enough to attract the driver's attention. When he looked at me, I flashed my badge and said, "Pull over." After that, whenever I visited their office, at least one of the youth services officers would say, "Here comes old Woo Woo."

On one such visit, I was waiting to ride with one of the detectives when the police dispatcher advised of an armed robbery of a nearby grocery store. Today, robberies are as common as fleas on a dog, but back then they were extremely rare and would make the front page of the local newspaper, often for days. A description of the getaway vehicle was broadcast, and all of the detectives, wanting to be part of the action, ran for their cars, leaving me to answer the phone. There was a police-band radio monitor in the office, so even though I couldn't go with them (dammit), I was able to keep tabs on the hunt for the robbers.

In a few minutes, a motorcycle officer radioed that he had found the suspect vehicle parked in front of a house on the north side of town and would be investigating. Hearing nothing more from the officer for a minute or so, the dispatcher began calling his unit number. No response. After several unanswered pages, Chief Earl White got on the radio and said, "Forget the robbers, find that officer!" In about another minute, the frantic voice of another officer announced, "I found him. Send an ambulance, he's been shot!" There was a brief pause, then the same officer said, "Hold the ambulance, he's not shot after all." Another short delay, then the obviously confused officer said, "Better send the ambulance, he doesn't know whether he's shot or not."

This was early winter, and the motorcycle officer was wearing a thick leather jacket. Turns out he had walked behind the house in front of which he had located the vehicle, and just as he rounded a rear corner, one of the perpetrators had stepped out from behind an outbuilding and emptied his pistol in the direction of the officer. Startled, needless to say, the officer fell backward onto his butt and also emptied his pistol (and, more than likely, his bowels). Twelve shots were fired, and nobody was hit.

Don't get me wrong, I'm not making fun of anybody. As I mentioned earlier in this chapter, I've been shot at, and to say that's a stressful situation would be the understatement of the year. Lots of people who can shoot holes in paper targets with remarkable accuracy don't perform as well when the target is shooting back.

Take the case of Deputy Sheriff Mike Arnold. He accompanied the chief of police in a nearby town to a residence in an attempt to locate a female juvenile who had been reported as a runaway. The chief had received information that this girl was staying at an address with two young men. While Arnold and the chief were searching the house for this girl, one of the boys stepped out of a closet and shot the chief in the head, killing him instantly. Mike returned fire, striking the perpetrator twice. Also accompanying Mike and the chief on their search was an officer from another jurisdiction. Hearing the gunfire, he stepped into the room and emptied his nine-millimeter pistol at the shooter—seventeen rounds at point-blank range—without striking him even once. Nerves? Yeah, you could say that.

It was pretty well-known in his agency that Mike was a switch hitter. That is, he admittedly liked to date both girls and boys, although being around him for just a brief period made it pretty clear that his preference was for members of his own sex. Now, I have always subscribed to a philosophy of live and let live. As long as his behavior was not illegal or detrimental to the overall functioning of our office, I really didn't care what Mike or anyone else did while off duty.

When word got out that Mike was leaving the sheriff's department and coming to work for us, there was much snickering and rumormongering going on in our office. One day, I chanced upon a gaggle of male officers who were making derogatory comments about Mike. I listened for a minute, then I said, "May I inject myself into this discussion?" Hearing no dissent, I continued, "When Mike Arnold gets here, he and I will be the only two officers in this office—at least as far as I know—who have ever been shot at. I know how I reacted, but more importantly, I know how Mike reacted. Frankly, I have no idea how you 'girls' would handle that situation. So with all due respect, the next dangerous arrest I have to make, I'm going to use Mike for backup. After all, he is a known quantity." End of discussion, and I am happy to report that Mike was graciously accepted as a member of our staff.

This may come as a shock to those who regard law enforcement as a macho profession, but increasingly, the thin blue line is being joined by admitted homosexuals. In fact, in a fifteen-officer parole office where I worked, we had three during one period: one male and two females. One of the lesbians, Trixie Atherton, was open about her sexual preference to the point of aggression. She would sit with some of the male officers, poring over pictures of nude females in, ahem, gentlemen's magazines.

Trixie had been married previously (to a man) and had a young child; however, for reasons known only to her, she had, at some point in her life, made a 180-degree turn. One day, she and I happened to be in the employee parking area at the same time, and I commented favorably on her personal vehicle, a black Mercedes. She thanked me, then she added, "It makes a great chick magnet." TMI (too much information), Trixie, TMI. Like I said, I believe in staying out of the personal lives of coworkers, so *leave* me out. Please!

David Eagan was really too hyper to be in law enforcement. He held an advanced belt in karate, but he also had a short fuse and was prone to decisions that were—um, how to say this politely—stupid. He and another parole officer went to a small motel in an attempt to arrest a parole violator. Before going to the man's room, they obtained a key from the motel manager. Good call—so far. Maintain the element of surprise, giving the arrestee less time to respond violently. Well, David very quietly unlocks the room door then throws it open. At that precise moment, a large dog appeared from behind the bed and ran toward the two officers.

Now, you know how small the average motel room is, right? Point being that this poor dog could not have been more than eight or ten feet away. Needless to say, David was startled by the unexpected appearance of this animal, so guess what? He shoots at him—and misses! The parolee was not present, so David and helper return to the office empty-handed and red-faced. Especially when they have to present a written account of the fiasco to their supervisor. He goes out to the room the following day and encounters the same dog, who he says approached in a friendly manner, just wanting to be petted. I just had to dig David a little, so I said, "You know, David, if I had fired at a target that large at point-blank range and missed, I don't think I would have admitted it."

When I was a police officer, one our best in-service training sessions was designated Armed Offender Confrontation. We were taken to an old school building, no longer in use, and required to sit, without talking, in a classroom. The whole time, there was antipolice rap playing over a speaker. At one point, the lights suddenly went out, and somebody fired an automatic weapon nearby. Then, the real fun began.

One by one, we were escorted by a "handler" into the school hallway, which was dimly lit and occupied by actors grabbing at us, threatening us with violence, and urging, "Shoot! Shoot!" Of course, no live ammunition was used, but we did have our sidearm, loaded with blanks. In rapid succession, with no time to decompress or assimilate what had just happened, we were taken by our escort into ten different classrooms. In each, a scenario had been staged to replicate a situation where a police officer had actually been killed. We had to decide whether—and when—to shoot, or we might be "killed" ourselves. The last confrontation occurred in the hallway, where a "bad guy" stepped out from behind a partition and unloaded a double-barreled shotgun toward us. This one happened so fast you had no time to react. You just "died."

At the end of the session, we were ushered into a cool-down room where we were given cookies and soft drinks and allowed to get our blood pressure back within an acceptable range. Realistic? Well, we had a female officer who became so hysterical she had to be transported to the local emergency room and a male officer who peed in his pants. His uniform pants. The same ones he had to wear for the rest of his shift.

No matter how experienced you are, the sight of a person with a firearm will definitely increase your pucker factor. One day I was making some required home visits, checking on the whereabouts and behavior of my parolees. One of them, a small middle-aged alcoholic named Artie Davis, had reported moving to a new address, so I went there to verify that he was actually staying there. I drove down the dead-end street without seeing the address Artie had reported, so I backed into a man's driveway, intending to return to the main street.

Seeing me, the resident came up to my car to ask if he could help me. Now, visualize this, if you will. I am sitting in my car, which is parked perpendicular to the street. As I look east up the street, I see Artie staggering toward my car. In itself, this was no cause for alarm; however, I observed that he was holding by his side a small semiautomatic pistol. I advised the helpful resident that he might want to get the hell out of the way, then I drew my own gun, holding it just below the car's window ledge, out of Artie's sight. When he got about twenty feet from my vehicle, I raised my weapon, pointed it at him, and said, "That's close enough, Artie!"

Artie proceeded to drop his gun, which, from the sound it made as it bounced off the asphalt roadway, I quickly ascertained was a plastic toy. I called Artie over to my car, and he said, "I was just coming to show you it was a toy." Apparently, he had been trying to intimidate the neighbors, and he believed they had reported him to me. What I told Artie was less than polite; it involved words like *stupid*, *dumbass*, and *death*. As I drove away from the scene in search of the nearest bathroom, I solved potential future problems by running over Artie's gun. The sound of the plastic being crunched beneath my tires was satisfying.

Then there was Jimmy Daniels. Jimmy was a convicted arsonist. Like most arsonists, he received sexual gratification by watching things burn. He was on parole from a sentence received for torching a house. When arrested, he told investigators that he did not set the fire. He said that he was walking to work when he saw a house on fire. According to Jimmy, he kept walking, fearing that he would be blamed for starting the fire. Then he came upon a field on fire. Once again, he kept walking. He soon passed by another field on fire, at which point he was detained by neighborhood residents, who told police they had observed him starting the fire. Now, in all the years I spent as a police patrol officer, I never discovered even one fire, much less three in one day.

Anyway, Jimmy had committed a violation of parole, and I went to his residence to arrest him. He requested permission to retrieve a pair of socks from a bureau drawer. My mind must have been on a temporary vacation because I said okay. As he reached into the drawer, my alertness returned. I'm glad it did. I was already drawing my weapon when I saw Jimmy beginning to turn toward me—holding a gun in his hand! As he got about ninety degrees into his turn, he stopped and said, "It's a pellet gun." By this time, I had my pistol pointed directly at his left temple. I replied, "This one isn't."

Even the possibility that you may have to face an armed adversary causes the apprehension level to increase dramatically. One day I had gone to a low-income minority neighborhood to interview residents concerning their opinion of a man on whom I was performing a presentence investigation. As I mention in another part of the book, people in certain neighborhoods tend to view a man in a suit with some suspicion. They figure he is either a cop or a bill collector. Knowing this, I realized many years ago that, discretion being the better part of valor, it is wise to maintain as low a profile as possible when in these areas. Go in, do your business, get out. Anyway, it was a hot summer day, and most of these homeowners had no air-conditioning. As a result, they left their windows and doors open in order to catch any available breeze.

As I walked onto the porch of one house, I noticed that the front wooden door was open and only the screen door was closed. I knocked on the door, and here's what I heard next: "LOOK OUT, YOU FOOL! HE'S GOT A GUN." Expecting an armed confrontation at any moment, I drew my pistol and flattened my back against the wall adjacent to the door. At about this time, an elderly woman answered my knock. Seeing me against her wall, holding a gun, she chuckled and said, "You gonna think I'm crazy. I was talking to the TV." Holy crap, Batman!

Guns aren't the only weapons that can scare the poop out of you. My first year as a probation and parole officer was spent in an old Southern city with neighborhoods close to town that dated back to the nineteenth century. One day I was looking for a female parolee named Brandy LaTour. Brandy had not run away, at least not so far as I knew, but she had moved without permission, and I needed to find her. I received information from an informant that she was staying at 555 St. Anthony Street, one of those turn-of-the-century areas.

So I drove alone (first mistake) to St. Anthony Street. By the time I was a block away from number 555, I could hear the jukebox blaring. It was that loud. I drove up to 555 St. Anthony and determined that the music was coming from that house. More importantly, there was a metal soft drink sign hanging on the front of the home identifying it as Booker T.'s Guest House.

If you have read this far, you have probably ascertained that I am a Christian. I believe totally in God, and I know that He loves me and will protect me. I also know that He has a sense of humor. Look at the giraffe and tell me otherwise. So I drove around the block laughing. I said, "Hey, God, good joke. But I know you wouldn't want me to go into a place like that. Right? Right, God? You were just pulling my leg, weren't you?" Well, guess what? When I got back to 555, it was still Booker T.'s Guest House. Now, we had no radios to call for backup, and cell phones had not been invented in 1971. A prudent man would have returned to his office and brought another officer or two with him. I'm not always prudent.

The house was a two-story frame dwelling that appeared to have been built sometime around 1900. In keeping with its Victorian style, the front door fed into a long hallway, with rooms on either side. The music was emanating from the first room on the right, so I peered cautiously around the doorframe. And what to my wondering eyes should appear? No, it wasn't Santa Claus and eight tiny reindeer. In the middle of this large bare room was a table, around which were seated five of the biggest black dudes I have ever seen. I'm six foot one and weigh about two hundred, but these guys made me look puny. On the table were cards, money, three large knives, and a gallon jug of moonshine. During the instant it took me to take in all these criminal violations, one of the players had spotted me. In a voice that sounded like thunder, he said, "WHAT YOU WANT?"

I really don't like being challenged by law violators, even when the odds are against me. Still, I made an instant assessment of the situation. I had a .38 caliber revolver holding six cartridges, and I figured that the size these men were, it would probably take three shots to bring just one of them down. So I answered, "Um, nothing. Just leaving." As I started toward the front door, I saw Brandy coming down the stairs from the second floor. Between clenched teeth, I hissed, "Get your ass out on the sidewalk." I gave her until sundown that day to present me with a more acceptable home plan. Then, without further ado, I left.

Equipment (Brain) Failure

Radios are not the only items of equipment that can cause police officers trouble. Probably the funniest, um, *malfunctions* occur with firearms. Yes, you heard right: firearms. But aren't cops supposed to be experts at handling guns? Well, you be the judge.

Except when we charged someone with a felony, our arrests were tried in the municipal court. There was a lounge area for officers who were not testifying, and in that room were several metal boxes capable of being locked. Prior to entering the courtroom, an officer was required to remove his firearm and lock it in one of these boxes. It was not unusual for the officer, upon leaving the courtroom, to forget his or her pistol, necessitating a return trip to the court building. If you were too far away when you noticed your lapse of memory, it was prudent to advise dispatch that you were returning to court so that they would not try to send you, unarmed, on a call.

At times, life in the 911 center was mundane to the point of terminal boredom, and when it was like this, dispatchers would do anything (almost) to relieve the monotony—like saying, "Forget something?" This would frequently provoke other officers to interject something funny, like "Oops" or "Hee haw." Generally, though, this forgetfulness caused no serious problem—that is, unless you did not notice your weapon was missing until after the court building was closed. This happened to one of our officers, and it might not have created a problem had he not been dispatched to back me up on a call of a robbery in progress. We arrived at the scene at the same time, and he said, "Hey, man, I left my gun at court. Do you have a shotgun?" I just shook my head and said, "Go around back. If the perpetrator runs out, point your finger at him." Fortunately, the call was a false alarm.

A similar situation occurred while I was stationed in the western part of the state as a parole officer. One day I received a call from Jerry Abrams. Jerry was a just a few years younger than I, and he was the police chief in one of the county's small towns. Very small. In fact, the police force consisted of Jerry and one other officer (the assistant chief, I guess). Well, anyway, Jerry informed me that one of my parolees had attempted to rob the convenience store in town. Yes, *the* convenience store. The one just past *the* red light. If you are from a small town, you'll understand.

This parolee was definitely not a rocket scientist. His disguise was a stocking cap pulled down over his face. Not the kind skiers use, with eye and mouth holes. This was just a plain stocking cap. How he could even see, I have no idea. At any rate, he stuck one hand in his jacket pocket, pretending to have a weapon, and announced, "This is a robbery." I'm sure the store clerk knew exactly what was happening, but he pretended that the hat was muffling the parolee's voice, making him impossible to understand. After a couple more unsuccessful attempts, the robber pulled the hat up, exposing his face. Now, to make this really funny, he, along with most of the town's residents, was a regular customer of the store, and the clerk knew his name. Believe it or not, I actually had some clients who were that stupid. Well, Chief Abrams checked the guy's name and found out he was on parole, but he had no address for the perp. I did, so I volunteered to come to town and assist him with the arrest.

As we pull up near Bubba's mobile home, Jerry gives me this sheepish look and delivers some shocking news: "I don't have a gun." It took me a second to assimilate the news that this town's top cop did not have a weapon with him, then I asked, "Why not?" He said, "Umm...I forgot it." I was pretty sure that the occupants of the trailer had already seen us, and returning to the office for Jerry to arm himself would have given Joe Parolee time to hightail it.

So we went to the door and were met by the client's mother, who didn't want to allow us inside. After being informed that I would be happy to take her to jail along with her son, she relented. We started down the home's hallway toward the bedrooms, I with pistol drawn, Jerry cowering behind me. As we approached one of the bedrooms, I saw in a wall mirror the parolee hiding behind a bed. I explained to him in no uncertain terms that we were there to arrest him and that if I saw any part of his body before I saw his empty hands, he would be meeting that great parole board in the sky. He surrendered peacefully, and we transported him to jail.

As I was leaving to return to my office, I looked at Jerry and said, "Jerry, I like you, but this ain't 1960, and you're not in Mayberry."

In one office where I worked as a parole and probation officer, we had a very small suite of offices on the fifth floor of the county courthouse. Directly across the hall from our offices was a public bathroom, used by us for the usual purpose and also for conducting drug tests on probationers and parolees. One of our younger officers was a guy named Lomax Edwards. Lomax was a small man, probably not over five six standing on tiptoe. Well, one day, Lomax announced that he was going across the hall to take a, um, break. If you have ever worn a pistol on your waist, you know that you must remove it before dropping your drawers, as the gun weighs three or four pounds, making it darn nigh impossible to pull your pants back up while wearing it. Since Lomax had plenty of time to prepare for his visit to the potty, it would have been wise of him to have removed his weapon and locked it in his desk. He didn't. Instead, he removed his gun while in the bathroom stall then forgot it. Remember, this was a public bathroom, frequented not only by us but by our clients as well.

Disaster was averted when the next visitor to that stall, a county probation officer, found Lomax's pistol and, knowing that this was the type and caliber of weapon we were assigned, brought it into the office. Lomax, however, did not avoid embarrassment. Our head secretary yelled out, "OKAY, WHO LEFT HIS GUN IN THE CRAPPER?"

Of all the people who should be proficient in the handling of firearms and constantly aware of the dangers they pose, police officers come to mind first. But stress can cause even the most experienced officers to do some things they later regret.

Take the case of Sandra Simmons, a veteran officer who, during a routine pat-down of a suspect, discovered a .25 caliber semiautomatic pistol in his pocket. These guns are cheap and are frequently referred to, along with small .22 caliber revolvers, as Saturday night specials. This appellation comes from the fact that the road to hell is reportedly paved with people who have been killed by one of these guns during a disagreement, frequently alcohol-fueled and often on a weekend night. Well, anyway, before handcuffing her suspect, Officer Simmons stuck the confiscated weapon in a rear pocket of her uniform pants. Now, as I said, these guns are cheap and usually don't have any kind of safety device to prevent an accidental discharge. When she sat down in her patrol car—you guessed it—the weapon fired, striking Officer Simmons in the left cheek of her ample buttocks. She survived the wound, but of course, this story made the rounds, and her pride suffered a serious injury.

About two o'clock one morning, I was dispatched to meet several other officers at the city's oldest mall. Responding to a burglar alarm, officers had climbed to the roof of the mall and captured one burglar, who was seated in a patrol car by the time I arrived; however, they had reason to believe that one or more perpetrators might still be on the roof, and they wanted me to join the officers already up there to assist in a search.

Now, I suffer from a serious case of acrophobia (fear of heights). If I could have been magically transported to the roof, I would have been fine. But the only roof access was via a ladder attached to the side of the building. As I surveyed that ladder, I felt my vertigo kick in, and I knew there was no way I could climb it. So I was told to remain on the ground and relieve the officer who was guarding the prisoner already in custody. He then took my place and climbed up to the roof.

Maybe five minutes had elapsed when I heard three gunshots in rapid succession. Shortly thereafter, a gaggle of police officers began climbing down from the roof, and all of them were laughing heartily—all except one, that is. Marty Lane's face wore an expression that can best be described as a mixture of bewilderment and humiliation. It seems that Marty, the officer who had earlier relieved me, was walking across the roof with the other officers, all of whom had drawn their weapons in preparation for a possible confrontation with the burglary suspects.

If you have ever been on the roof of a commercial building, you know that on some are several large structures, such as elevator motor housings and commercial air-conditioners. Marty had just passed one of these huge air-conditioning units when it turned on with a loud *whoosh*. Unfortunately, its life came to a sudden and tragic end. Marty was so startled by this loud noise directly behind him that he turned and fired three shots at it, effectively neutralizing the "threat." Between the ribbing he was taking and the assurance from the other officers that he was going to be required to pay for this large expensive compressor, I thought the poor kid was going to cry.

You have probably heard the old saying, "Familiarity breeds contempt." This is true for firearms as much as for any other type of machinery, and unfortunately, cops are just as likely to bear witness to this truth as the next person.

We were not issued shotguns; however, if you wanted, you could go to the back counter, designated Property and Evidence, prior to the beginning of your shift and check one out. These weapons were old and decrepit, but they did function—sometimes too well. One officer, ending his shift, brought the shotgun that he had checked out earlier back to Property and Evidence and, with a grand flourish, said, "Here, take this piece of crap!" Whereupon he slammed the gun down, butt-first, on the counter.

Now, almost all modern firearms have an internal safety mechanism that prevents the weapon from firing unless the trigger is pulled—*almost* all. Shotguns are the exception. Force a shell back against the firing pin with sufficient velocity and it will fire, whether the trigger is engaged or not. This officer had made three mistakes, and the last of the three was clearly the worst. First, he had failed to unload the shotgun. Secondly, he was playing with a weapon, which is a no-no, even if you are sure that the gun is unloaded. But his final mistake was a real doozey.

The weapon fired, blowing a large hole in the ceiling. Now that in itself was bad. *Very* bad. But I suspect that that act of negligence could have—and would have—been glossed over with a quick ceiling patch job, except for one major problem. I say major, because just above Property and Evidence was the office of one of the department's majors. This major had a private bathroom. Notice I said *had*. The double-aught buckshot made a square hit on his toilet, blowing it to smithereens! About the only thing that could have made the situation worse was if the accident had occurred during daylight hours, which might have found the major *sitting* on his throne.

Not all mishaps with property involve firearms. One night I was dispatched to a railroad crossing to investigate an accident. Dispatch advised me that this was a single-vehicle accident involving a police unit. Upon arrival, I discovered that the driver, Officer Vittorio "Vito" Vincente, had been approaching this railroad crossing when he observed the warning lights begin to flash. This crossing was of two sets of tracks running parallel to each other. Vito looked and saw that the approaching train was on the far set of tracks, so, for reasons known only to him, he pulled right up to the edge of those tracks – placing him squarely on the other set of tracks! Unfortunately, he had neglected to account for the wooden arm designed to keep traffic from crossing the tracks. It descended on his brand-new take-home vehicle, smashing his blue light and leaving a rather pronounced dent in the car's roof. After I stopped laughing, I said, "Vito, were you born stupid, or did you have to practice?" Vito was not amused.

Of course, I never made dumb mistakes. Well, not too often, anyway. Like the time I locked my keys in my car. Yes, my patrol car. See, when we exited our vehicles on a call, we liked to leave them unlocked. That way, if we had to reenter the car in a hurry or shove an unruly prisoner into the back seat, we didn't have to fumble around trying to unlock the door. However, on this particular occasion, I had been called to a small business in an unsavory area of town and realized that I might be out of sight of my unit for several minutes. Concerned that someone might, ahem, *borrow* something from my car, I locked the door. Good thinking: that is, if I had remembered to remove my key from the ignition first.

Upon my return to the vehicle, I realized my error. I borrowed a coat hanger from a nearby establishment and began trying, unsuccessfully, to unlock the door. After a few minutes, I was approached by a young male who said, "Officer, if you won't ask me any questions, I'll open that door for you." Now, understand my predicament: safety was not an issue. If I had gotten my butt in a sling, all I would have had to do was use my handheld radio to call for help. No, I wasn't worried about being temporarily stranded in a high-crime area. But I *was* scared—petrified, actually. Because I just *knew* that my dispatcher was going to try to send me on another call, and I would have to respond that I was unavailable—because my keys were locked in my car. I would *never* have lived that one down.

But would I, an upstanding, fearless, unimpeachable defender of truth, justice, and the American way, actually collaborate with this, this *criminal* just to avoid a little embarrassment? Bet your rear end I did! I handed him my hanger and turned my back, and in about ten seconds, he had me ready to rock and roll. Boy was earning some brownie points for future contact, but that was okay by me.

My hand-and-eye coordination is practically nil, and I have never been good at opening car doors with a coat hanger. Except once. I was off duty and wearing jeans, and I came out of a grocery store to find a woman who had locked her keys in her old Ford and was attempting to hook the door lock button with a bent metal hanger. She asked if I could help her, and I noticed that she was about an inch away from success. I took the hanger from her and almost immediately had the door unlocked. The grateful driver looked at me in amazement and asked, "What do you do? Are you a locksmith?" Just as serious as a heart attack, I replied, "No, actually I'm a professional car thief."

Being locked out of your car can be embarrassing and inconvenient. Being locked *inside* one can be downright scary. As I mention in another chapter, I am almost fanatical about neatness. I liked a neat, clean uniform, and I kept my patrol car the same way. Unless it was raining or there was some other circumstance beyond my control, I absolutely would not go on duty in a dirty car. One day I was working second shift and was scheduled to report for work at three o'clock in the afternoon. About noon, I was tidying up my ride in the driveway of my home. I had climbed into the back seat in order to clean the rear window. For whatever reason (probably devilment), my four-year-old son decided that it would be amusing to close the door, with me inside.

Now, to appreciate my situation, you have to know how our patrol cars were set up. Between the front and rear seats, there was a metal panel extending from the floor to the top of the front seat. Behind the driver was a sheet of clear plastic to prevent a prisoner from spitting on the driver (hopefully). Behind the front passenger seat was wire mesh to keep the little darlings from suffocating. The inside handles had been removed from the rear doors and replaced with a piece of sheet metal. In other words, the back seat was virtually escape proof. And that was where I was. My son was outside the car, laughing gleefully. I tried everything: begging, pleading, wheedling, cajoling, bargaining, and threatening.

My biggest concern was that if I failed to report for work and my headquarters could not raise me by phone, they would send a unit to my house to check on me and find me locked in my own damn car! Somehow I managed to convince my child of the folly of his behavior, and he released me. I determined that I would allow him to live until his next birthday, at which time I would reassess his value to humanity. Hey, lighten up. He's in his thirties now and married. No kids yet. Too bad. Grandpa has some great ideas for things they can do to—I mean, *with*—daddy.

I will have to say that I have always had a great respect for the potential of firearms to inflict harm, and I am very cautious when handling them. Still, even I am subject to mistakes occasionally. My first wife was originally from the southern part of our state, and her parents still lived there when we got married. They had a small farm way out in the country. My father-in-law raised a few head of cattle and always maintained about two acres in fresh vegetables. On and all around their homestead, there was an abundance of wildlife. Drive just a few miles along their farm-to-market road and you might see deer, turkey, dove, and quail, to say nothing of road kill like opossums, raccoons (otherwise known to us Southern boys as possums and coons), and armadillos. In fact I hunted dove and quail on their land on a number of occasions.

Well, one time, my wife and I were en route for a visit, and as we were driving down the road, I saw a wild turkey hen just standing beside the pavement. Now, it wasn't turkey season, but let me assure you, if you have not tasted it, that a properly prepared wild turkey is some seriously good eating. In season or not, I decided I would kill this hen and take her to my mother-in-law to cook. Since all game were out of season at this time of year, I didn't have a shotgun with me. However, I did have my service weapon, a .357 magnum revolver. I brought the car to a quick stop, and before the turkey had time to flee in alarm, I rested my pistol on the vehicle's window ledge and fired.

In case you don't know, please take it from someone who does (now): the majority of the noise caused by a bullet fired from a revolver does not come from the barrel. No, it is created within the frame of the gun—and that part of my pistol was still inside my car. Boys and girls, don't try this at home. I can tell you from sad experience that your hearing will never be quite the same. Actually, at that moment, my hearing loss was somewhat of a blessing, as I could not fully hear my wife, who was calling me everything but a child of God. Until then I never knew that she had such an extensive vocabulary of epithets. Of course, before we divorced, I got to hear all of them again—many times.

Oh, and just in case you're wondering, I *missed* the stinking turkey.

Firing ranges can provide an almost inexhaustible variety of anecdotes. Ever seen the old newsreel footages that document the early years of the FBI? Almost invariably, they contain images of agents on the firing range using their old .38s, that era's pistol du jour, in an efficient and professional manner. Yeah. Too bad they don't also show you the outtakes.

When I was a parole officer, we never maintained a range of our own. Instead, we would conduct our annual pistol qualification sessions on a range we had borrowed from some other agency. In one office where I worked, we were allowed to use the facility belonging to the local police department. This was a nice, well-maintained range, but it did have one inherent deficiency: its location. It was under the municipal football stadium, and aside from the dirt backstop into which we fired, it was fashioned entirely of concrete. Loud? You don't know loud.

Anyway, one day we had to shoot there. At the time, the state had not issued us firearms, so we were carrying our own. I was on the far right end of the firing line with my weapon of choice, a .45 automatic. On my left was a young officer, Tom Milford, who was preparing to shoot his pistol, a nine millimeter. Now I know that all the gang bangers and wannabe thugs think a nine millimeter is the greatest thing since sliced bread, but I would just about as soon have David's slingshot. I have read too many stories of law enforcement officers having to shoot an offender seven or eight times with a nine before he was finally incapacitated. In addition to being what I consider an ineffective man stopper, the report a nine makes is fairly mild—at least, compared to my hand cannon. I looked at Tom and said, "Tom, this is a .45, and it will be loud. Okay?" He nodded as though he understood. He didn't.

When firing the FBI pistol proficiency course (PPC), I always liked to squeeze off a round as soon as I cleared leather, since I knew that would be required in a real shooting, which I was trying to simulate as closely as possible. So the whistle blew to signal us to fire, I drew my big old auto, and *kaboom*! The noise was clearly much louder than Tom was expecting. He jumped about a foot in the air and fired his first shot. Unfortunately, while jumping up, he had also pointed his pistol toward the floor. His shot ricocheted off the floor then the ceiling. After the first round of fire, he said, "Are you sure that damn thing is legal?" I just smiled.

On another occasion, we were at the same range, when I pulled one that really should have been captured on film for one of these funniest videos television shows.

We were in the last course of fire for the PPC course. In this exercise, you stand almost touching the target and fire six rounds, one-handed. Then you switch your pistol to the other hand and fire six more rounds. You'd think it would be virtually impossible to miss the target at this range, wouldn't you? Think again. I had suffered a jam when firing with my right hand. An empty cartridge had failed to properly eject from my gun, rendering it inoperable. There is a procedure for clearing such a malfunction, but it takes a few seconds. My allotted time for this part of the course had almost elapsed by the time I shifted my weapon to my left hand, so I had to squeeze off my rounds about as fast as my gun would cycle. As I fired my last shot, I felt a burning sensation on my left arm near the elbow.

Now, if you have ever been near another person firing a semiautomatic pistol, you know that spent rounds are ejected from a pistol with some force and can actually come over and strike you. Having just been filled with burning gunpowder, they are hot as the hinges of hell. I have had one down my shirt and actually had one land on the bridge of my nose between my glasses and my face—and get stuck there (pro that I am, I kept shooting). So I'm thinking this was just an empty shell from the shooter next to me. That is, until I looked down and saw a small stream of blood trickling down my arm. Almost simultaneously, the range officer Gary Shine walked up to me and said, "Do you want this?" He opened his hand to reveal a .45 caliber bullet.

This round was lead, covered by a full copper jacket. It was obvious that the round had ricocheted, as the metal jacket was torn partially off the lead. This was what had hit my arm, after bouncing off the concrete floor and ceiling of the range just like Tom Milford's bullet had. After cutting me, the bullet had continued on its path, striking Shine in the leg. Fortunately, he was wearing jeans, so all he got was a bruise. I looked at the ragged projectile, and he repeated, "Do you want it or not?" I smiled sheepishly and replied, "Depends on where you're planning to put it."

We had one parole officer named C. T. Samuels. CT absolutely did not like guns, and attempting to explain the proper functioning of one to him was akin to trying to make me comprehend physics. I don't, never have, and never will. Moreover, I really don't care.

Well, that was CT's attitude toward firearms. One day we were at a firing range where ten people could shoot at once. Several of us, including CT, were behind the firing line loading our pistols while awaiting our turn to shoot. Suddenly, CT's pistol discharged. Fortunately, he had it pointed at the ground at the time. CT claimed that the weapon had malfunctioned. He said that as he released the slide on the semiauto to feed a round into the firing chamber, it just went off. The range officer cycled about twenty rounds through the gun, attempting to duplicate the problem. It functioned perfectly each time. It was pretty obvious to all assembled that CT had carelessly been squeezing the pistol's trigger when he released the slide, causing it to fire. But until the day he retired, CT swore that his gun had malfunctioned.

Jokers Wild

Humor may not be something you learn in the police academy, but it sure helps make the stress and pathos of the job easier to take.

During the 1970s, I was working as a probation and parole officer. My agency decided to experiment with the use of halfway houses designed for probationers who had committed minor violations of probation and prisoners being paroled from the penitentiary with no community resources, such as a home and job. The idea was to help these clients get on their feet, then place them back into the community in regular probation or parole supervision. I was promoted to a supervisory position and appointed director of one of the three facilities.

At the time of my appointment, the facility itself was only a concept. It was my duty to find and lease a building that would be acceptable to both the parole board and the community. Once that was accomplished, I had to make such changes as were necessary to satisfy the various city inspectors (fire, health, zoning, etc.). I then selected a staff composed of an assistant director, who was also an experienced probation and parole officer, a secretary, and four house parents. Actually, the title house parent was a little misleading: they did not live on premise but worked an assigned eight-hour shift, with the fourth being the relief person for whichever other one was off duty at the time.

My assistant was an officer by the name of Joe White. Joe was known to consume a rather large quantity of adult beverages during his off time, and as a result, he frequently appeared for work at 8:00 a.m. looking like he had been run over by a truck. Not a large truck that would kill you, more like a pickup that just screws you up for life. Things were a little slow, so I suggested to my secretary and morning houseparent that we have a little fun with Joe.

We knew him to be a creature of habit: he would come in each morning in a blue haze and head directly to the dining room, where he would reach into the built-in cupboard for his cup and pour himself some coffee. My secretary brought to work a rubber hand, one of those grisly things you see at Halloween, with blood all over it and muscle tissue trailing out the back. We placed it in the cupboard and waited. Sure enough, Joe arrived, hung over as usual, and made a beeline for the cupboard. There was a very lengthy pause, after which he stumbled into the office, clearly shaken and muttering something like "Uhh…uhhh…HAND…uhhh." It was too funny for words.

You know what they say about payback? Well, I was sure Joe would do something to get even, but several days went by with no retribution, and I pretty much forgot the whole thing. Of course, like Joe, I was also a creature of habit. My morning routine was to go directly to my office, open the middle drawer of my desk, and place my pistol there. Well, one morning, I opened the drawer and discovered the biggest, blackest snake I had ever seen! I had drawn my weapon and was backing away from the desk, preparing to blow that snake to hell, when I realized that my coworkers were screaming, "No, no, don't shoot! It's rubber." Don't know how I would have explained that one to the parole board.

I was fairly well-known as a practical joker, and I was always on the alert for somebody trying to turn the tables on me and make me the victim of a prank. One day, at the halfway house, all of our residents had left for work, and there really wasn't much for any of us to do. My assistant, secretary, and houseparent had gathered around my desk, and we were playing a card game called spades (I know, I know, you're shocked that government workers would goof off, right?). The telephone rang, and since I was closest to it, I answered. A male caller greeted me with "Dr. Melton?" I was sure this was someone I knew being funny, so I answered, "Yes, this is Dr. Melton."

Well, come to find out, this was actually a classification officer from a federal penitentiary. Since our funding was by federal grant, the US Bureau of Prisons could utilize us as a contract facility, placing federal prisoners with us for the last two months of their sentence to help reassimilate them into the community. Of course, by now, it was too late to explain to this classification specialist that I was not really a Ph.D. I listened intently as he told me all about a potential resident, including information about the battery of psychological tests that had been administered to him, many of which I did not comprehend. Now, to really make this funny, you have to realize that I was still seated with my feet on my desk and devoting most of my attention to the card game. Occasionally, I would respond to the caller with "Mm hm" or "I see," just to make him think I was really paying attention.

After several minutes of giving me a verbal biography of this prisoner, the classification officer said, "Now, Dr. Melton, do you think that this individual would benefit from inclusion into the plans and programs of your facility?" I answered, "Yeah, put the dude on a Greyhound and send him on." Undoubtedly, this classification specialist suspected that a Ph.D would not have answered in such a cavalier fashion. He must have checked my credentials with my agency because the next time he called, he said, "Hey, Glenn, this is Nate in Tallahassee. I've got another dude for you."

My career as a probation and parole officer eventually led me back to a field office, where I had a regular caseload. One of my coworkers, Dan Packer, had an office right next to mine. Dan was sure that my practical jokes were going to send me directly to hell, without passing go or collecting my two hundred dollars, and that if he did not try to stop me, he would be condemned along with me. The boy had absolutely no sense of humor.

From where my office was located, I could not actually see the secretaries in the outer office, but I was close enough that I could hear everything that was said. One day, I heard a couple come to the front counter and ask to see the judge. Apparently, like many people, they did not understand the difference between probate and probation and had confused our office with that of the probate judge. The secretary explained that there were several judges in the courthouse and asked which one they wanted to see. Their response was "It don't matter, we just want to get married." Now this was in the days when three-piece suits with vests were popular. I was wearing a nice one and thought I looked particularly professional, and I could tell by their voices that this couple was young and unsophisticated (translation: ripe for a practical joke), so I walked out of my office with my thumbs hooked in my lapels, trying my best to appear "honorable," and announced, "Yes, dearly beloved, here I am." Packer ran out of his office and was on me like spots on dice and stink on—well, you know. I never knew until then that the boy could move so fast. He had a wild expression on his face and was waving his arms and shouting to the victims, er, couple—"RUN! RUN!"

Of course, they had no idea what the problem was, but they fled from the office like the devil himself was pursuing them. Packer gave me this contemptuous look and said, "You would really have done it, wouldn't you?" I said, "Why, hell yes. I've been down the aisle so many times I know the speech by heart." Plus, I knew that the judge whose office was located right next to ours was at lunch, so I could have used his courtroom. Packer folded his arms across his chest and said, "And I suppose you would have signed your name to the marriage certificate?" I replied, "Well, of course not. How stupid would that have been?" Packer smiled smugly, as though his intervention in this attempted devilment had caused me to see the error of my ways and thus be saved from eternal damnation. Wrong again. I continued, "Actually, I planned to sign *your* name."

Before Packer had completely realized my proclivity for pranks, he would occasionally accompany me on errands. One day, we were at the municipal court building waiting for a clerk to look up an arrest record on an individual when these two young guys approached the window. It was apparent that one of them was there to pay a fine, as he was holding a badly crumpled traffic ticket in one hand. He scrutinized the raggedy paper and told his companion, "I can't read this. I bet they ain't gonna be able to either." Again, I was wearing a nice suit and felt that I appeared very lawyerly, so I snatched the citation out of the fellow's hand and said, "Pardon me, young man, I happen to be an attorney-at-law. Permit me to examine this uniform traffic ticket and complaint." After "examining" it briefly, I announced, "Yes, this document is totally illegible."

By this time, Packer had turned his whole body away from us. He was sure Satan would appear momentarily to claim my soul, and he wanted to make it clear that he was not a part of this immoral activity. The victim then said, "I got another one just like it at home. You think I ought to go get it?" I looked out the front window of the court building, and to say that it was pouring would be the understatement of the year. Water was flowing ankle-deep in the streets, and these two rocket scientists were wearing old-fashioned high-top canvas tennis shoes.

The little angel seated on my right shoulder whispered in my ear, "Now, Glenn, you know that would be just wrong." About the same time, the little devil on my left shoulder said, "He don't know you vewy well, do he?" As the two boy geniuses left in the deluge, I could hear Packer muttering, "Not just GOING to hell, you're gonna ROT there." He was not a particularly religious person, but I do believe that if he had had access to a rosary, he would still be saying Hail Marys.

When the parole board was considering whether to parole an inmate, they would send to the field office that supervised the area where he planned to live a document called a parole plan. This outlined the inmate's proposed home and employment proposals, which were then checked by a parole officer to be sure they were legitimate. For many years before I retired, the workload had become so heavy that these plans were usually verified by telephone. However, early in my career, we used to actually make a personal visit, at least to the proposed home, before reporting our findings to the parole board.

On one such occasion, I found myself at an apartment in a federally subsidized housing project. My knock at the door was answered by a late-teens female. I did not identify myself to this young woman but asked to speak with her mother, who was the head of the household. Now, people in these projects tend to be suspicious of men in suits, thinking they are either bill collectors or cops. Because of that, they will often lie. Accordingly, when I asked for her mother, this teenager replied, "She ain't here." I was pretty sure she wasn't being truthful, so I said, "That's too bad. See, I'm from the parole board, and I wanted to talk to her about getting her son out of prison."

Boy, did that change things! This was a townhouse-style (two-story) apartment, and daughter turned and yelled up the stairs, "Mama, the parole man's here." Down the stairs came mama, who informed me that, of course, sonny could live with her. I was in the mood for a little mischief (when was I not?), so I said, "Well, ma'am, I'm afraid I won't be able to let him live here." Big tears popped in her eyes, and she asked, "Why not, mister?" I replied, "One of his parole conditions will be that he can't associate with people of disreputable or harmful character [this was true], and your daughter just lied to me. I'd say that makes her disreputable, wouldn't you?"

I had looked down at the inmate's file when my peripheral vision picked up something moving—fast. I looked up just in time to see mama slap daughter across the face so hard that I thought she had cold cocked her. Daughter staggered back a couple of steps, then she fixed her mother with a look of disbelief. The unspoken message was clear: "What the hell? You're the one who told me to lie." Her mother then gave me a very earnest look and vowed, "She won't do that no more, mister." As I attempted, without much success, to stifle a smile, I reassured mama that I would approve the home plan.

The officer-in-charge of my office was a retired Army colonel named Frank Sharp. Frank liked to walk down to a local cafeteria for lunch, a distance of about two blocks. Trouble was, like me, he could look at the sun and start sweating. One day, I saw him return from lunch, enter his office, and close the door. Now, our offices at that time were basically cubicles with doors. The walls did not touch either the ceiling or the floor, so when I saw Frank's pants bag on the floor, I realized that he had undone them to tuck in his shirttail. It just so happened that while Frank was at lunch, I had gone to a local novelty shop and had purchased a fake firecracker. This thing looked like a small stick of dynamite. It came with replaceable fuses that would burn just like real fireworks, but it contained no powder. I lit the thing, opened Frank's door, threw it in, hollered, "Look out, Frank!" and slammed the door shut.

At once, from inside the office came a loud *thump*, and Frank's feet disappeared from view. Now Frank was not a young man, and I feared that he had suffered a heart attack and had fallen across his desk. Obviously, this would have had a severely negative effect, not only on my continued employment but on my freedom as well. I jerked the door open and saw Frank. He had somehow made it to the other side of his desk (I think he vaulted it). He had dropped his pants to the floor, and he was standing with one ear against the wall, the index finger of his right hand in the other ear and his left hand cupping his crotch. When I was finally able to stop laughing, I said, "Frank, what the hell were you doing?" His reply was "Well, I figured you had gone crazy, and I didn't want to lose anything important."

Frank was the victim of a ring-tailed doozey of a joke coauthored by me and a fellow officer, Barry Broadstreet. Long before the national chicken restaurant chain devised their clever commercial ads around the phrase "Eat More Chicken," the cattlemen's association in the state where I worked had handed out automobile bumper stickers that read "Eat More Beef." Some wag decided to parody this advertising effort, which resulted in my coming into possession of a bumper sticker with the slogan "Eat More Possum." I showed this to Barry, and we determined that we could, without much effort, change this to read something really vulgar. I mean, we had the p, the u, and two s's, and very little talent was required to change the m to a y. So of course, that was just what we did.

Although we were quite pleased with our artistic creativity, we decided that the sticker would really not be funny unless it was displayed on somebody's car. Now Frank had this Cadillac, of which he was immensely proud. So Barry and I affixed our newly created sticker to his rear bumper. The next morning, Frank called me (why people always knew I was behind any prank was beyond me) into his office. He related that while he was driving home, several men had passed him, honking and giving him the thumbs-up sign of approval. Conversely, he was passed by a couple of women who gave him baleful stares. One even added a one-finger salute. He finally discovered the source of the attention and automatically assumed that I was involved. Fortunately, Frank was a joker himself and was able to appreciate the humor and our creativity.

As I said, Frank was not above pulling pranks of his own. On one such occasion, he and I had entered the elevator on the first floor of the county courthouse, which was where our office was. Our destination was the third floor, where all the judges' offices and courtrooms were located. The elevator stopped on the second floor, and a middle-aged woman got on. These elevators were as slow as cold molasses, and after the door closed, Frank passed gas—loudly. He never cracked a smile, but I did see a little tear forming in the corner of his eye. The hapless stranger never said a word, but her facial expression betrayed her fear. After all, she was confined to this small space with at least one lunatic. Frank pulled the same stunt on me in the menswear section of a nearby department store, but this time he said in a loud, reproachful voice, "Glenn! Shame on you!"

Frank was about sixty and had two half-grown sons, but he still had an eye for attractive women. In the early seventies, we had a suite of offices on the third floor of the county courthouse. All of our offices had one wall that was a bank of windows, so our view of the street below was expansive. In case you don't know, attorneys like to have their offices in close proximity to the local courthouse. Between court appearances and filing paperwork with the circuit court clerk, they spend a lot of time there, and being located close by means that they can walk rather than driving and having to look for a spot to park. We were happy to have so many attorneys close to our office, because each of them had at least one legal secretary who would make some trips to the courthouse in her boss's stead. Many's the time we have stood by the windows in our offices ogling the young miniskirted women as they sashayed down the street.

Well, Frank decided that we should institute a rating system for these young ladies. Depending on her looks, the victim of our lechery could score somewhere between one and ten, with ten being not only the highest score but a statistical impossibility. Sexist? Oh, hey, you bet. But before you criticize, ladies, just remember that we men know you look too. If you claim that you don't, remember this: you can go to hell for lying just as easily as you can for stealing.

So anyway, one day we're standing in our usual spot, mentally undressing every passing female, when we saw one that I knew personally. She was a real knockout, and Frank said, "Holy crap! There goes a nine if I ever saw one." I replied, "Frank, I know that girl, and believe me, she's as dumb as a rock. As soon as she opens her mouth, she drops to a three, and only that high because she's gorgeous." You'd have thought I had called Frank's wife a lady of the evening. He said, "Dammit, you can't do that. This is a looks-only rating. Adding personality totally screws it up." My answer was "Frank, I'm thinking about her as a date. And believe me, she's a space cadet."

About a year later, this same young lady was charged with a criminal offense, and I was assigned to conduct a presentence investigation on her for the sentencing judge. As she walked through the outer office to my cubbyhole, even our secretaries stopped and looked at her—she was that stunning. They would later confirm Frank's assessment that she was at least a nine. I began asking her for basic information that I would need for my report, and it was like trying to get information from a stone wall. She wasn't being uncooperative, she was just that dumb. As I mentioned earlier in this chapter, our office spaces were separated by wooden partitions that did not reach to the ceiling or the floor; therefore, my interview with her could easily be heard in Frank's office, which was adjacent to mine. It was the longest interview I ever took part in, and when she left, I was exhausted. I looked at Frank and said, "Believe me now?"

One of our district supervisors at the parole board was a middle-aged guy named Julius B. Walker. Some people called him Julius, others J.B. In addition to working for the state, Julius and his brother had made a substantial amount of money in the private sector. Knowing Julius, I'm sure that all these ventures were totally above board (read into that whatever you like). Anyway, Julius had invested part of his extra cash in a single-engine four-passenger Cessna airplane. When the parole board convened meetings of the district supervisors, Julius would fly his plane to a nearby private airport and call someone in our office to pick him up. Usually, this was Barry Broadstreet, to whom Julius was close.

On one of these occasions, I accompanied Barry on taxi duty, and when we took Julius back to the airport, we asked him for a brief flight. So into this little plane we all climb: Julius, Barry, and me. Now, I weigh around two hundred pounds, as did Julius; Barry was about two-fifty. In addition to all this heft, Julius had taken on a full load of fuel for his return trip. If you know much about personal aircraft, you have probably heard Cessnas referred to—derisively, of course—as lead sleds. That's because they are, well, let's just say, not overpowered. The result is that it takes a fairly long runway for them to attain takeoff speed.

With all the extra weight his plane was saddled with, it was taking Julius's plane longer than usual. *Way* longer. As we passed the point of no return, where braking was no longer possible and taking off was the only option, Julius announced, "I don't know if we're going to make it, fellas." Knowing his propensity for jokes, I assumed he was kidding. He wasn't. This little airport was out in the country. At the end of its short runway was an open field, and maybe a hundred yards farther, there was a large stand of mature pine trees. *Very tall* mature pine trees. As we cleared these trees, I heard a rather loud thump. I looked at Julius and asked, "What was that?" He replied, "Ah, we just clipped the top of one of those trees." Again, assuming he was messing with me, I laughed.

Ever been in a situation where you promised God that if He would get you out in one piece, you'd never do it again? That was what my flight with Julius was like. First, he got me and Barry distracted, then he eased back on the plane's "stick" imperceptibly without giving it more throttle. Of course, this caused our airspeed to drop. So low, in fact, that the stall warning—a loud horn—went off. I had just finished checking my pants for signs of an accident when Julius banked into a turn, again without increasing airspeed. Know what that does? It causes the tail of the aircraft to slide downward. Funny? Julius thought so. Finally, praise the Lord, we landed. As I was making my shaky exit from his plane, I saw a rather large pine bough stuck in one of the wheel struts. Julius had not been joking! We actually struck the top of a tree on takeoff. A foot lower and we would have died.

A couple of years later, Julius and I ran across a smaller and older Cessna for sale at a very reasonable price. He wanted us to go in together and buy it, but I brought up what I thought was a rather salient point. I said, "I don't know how to fly." Julius replied, "I'll teach you." I immediately hearkened back to my last flight with him and said, "No hell you won't! I promised God if He would let me out of that plane of yours, I would never fly with you again, and I ain't going back on my word."

I was somewhat surprised that Barry was not more alarmed during this flight than what he let on. He was a large imposing guy, but his bravery quotient was a little low, as I found out a couple of times. On one occasion, Barry had accompanied me in searching for a delinquent parolee. Our plan was to arrest him and take him to jail. I had the client's last known address, so we started there.

This was an old house near downtown, and it had been converted by the owner into a rooming house. Some of the residents, all elderly, were seated on the front porch when we arrived. As I stepped onto the porch, I saw an old black man seated to my right. I asked him, very politely, "How are you doing, sir?" His response, delivered very calmly but with definite self-assurance, was "I don't do to mess with. I know that." I actually did not hear him, so I said, "Excuse me?" He repeated what I'm sure was meant as a warning, but frankly, seeing his age and apparent physical infirmity, I thought it was sort of funny. I turned around smiling, expecting to see Barry. I saw him, all right. He had beat feet and was safely ensconced in our car.

Another time, I had Barry go with me in an attempt to locate and arrest General Lee Darcy. Back then, some people were named after celebrities or people of high social standing, and General was actually this parolee's first name. Over the years, I had Lawyer, Judge, and even Queen Elizabeth. But back to General. I was driving toward General's home address when I saw him standing in front of a washeteria to my left. So as not to spook him, I drove past. There was no place on this street to make a three-point turn. You know, where you turn about ninety degrees then back up. However, about two hundred yards past General's location, there was a large area of sand on the blacktop, apparently left when the road was repaired earlier.

I hit this sand at about forty-five miles per hour and, without warning Barry, slammed on the brakes and spun the steering wheel hard left. Per my plan, the car spun a little more than 180 degrees, leaving us pointing back to where General was standing. Barry talked about that maneuver for days, and it was some time before I could convince him to ride with me again.

Barry resigned from the parole board after a couple of years to accept a more lucrative government job. And that was probably a good thing because everything he and I ever collaborated on ended in disaster or had the potential to. One day I received information from an anonymous source that a delinquent parolee I had been looking for would be going to the local food stamp office. The caller said that the parolee would be dressed as an old woman and would be pretending to be a deaf mute.

So Barry and I hustled down to the food stamp office, but the parolee was nowhere to be found. On our way back to our office, I began to laugh. Barry wanted to know what was funny. Well, in those days, there were several beggars who hung around downtown. They would walk up and hand you a card that said, "Deaf mute, please help." I said, "Did it ever occur to you that we might have encountered a genuine deaf mute, and if so, what we might have done if she had reached in her purse for one of those cards?"

Then there was the time in 1972 when I had sold my house and was moving to another one I had bought. Barry volunteered—sort of—to help me load and unload my furniture. I decided that we weren't like Popeye, and spinach wasn't going to cut it. So I bought and iced down a case and a half of beer. I had also rented an eighteen-foot truck, which we proceeded to fill between stops to fill our bellies with beer. Now, Barry and I are both big guys; still, no matter how big you are or how hard you're working, half a case of beer is a skull popper. By the time we had emptied the truck, we were both blitzed.

I talked Barry into going with me to drop the truck off. I had left my car at the rental lot, and we were going to get in it and go do some *serious* partying. Anyway, we had driven a couple of blocks when I noticed in my rearview mirror that we were throwing up a wake of sparks. I looked at Barry and said, actually quite seriously, "Barry, either I left the tailgate down on this damn truck or we're being followed by a comet." Barry looked in the mirror on his side of the truck and declared that he thought it was, in fact, a comet, and we decided that we should try to outrun it.

So here we go, flying down the street, generating this huge trail of sparks and laughing like hell. God, if we had been stopped, we'd probably *still* be in jail. But we made it safely, I'm happy to report. The next workday, I was called at my office by the truck rental manager. The truck I had rented was almost new, and the tailgate had been painted a glossy black. Notice I said *had* been. It was now ground down to a raw steel sheen, which I personally thought was much more attractive. The manager asked if I knew what had caused the damage, and I feigned ignorance. It really wasn't anything that a couple of rattle cans of spray paint couldn't fix. Still…

Barry and I weren't the only two in our agency who could, and often did, quaff a substantial number of pop-tops. Each year, the parole board sponsored a conference, ostensibly to teach people new findings and theories that applied to our profession. Juvenile courts and social services offices from around the state also sent representatives. But frankly, few of our staff attended the meetings. We were too busy partying—or recovering from partying. I used to refer to the conference as a taxpayer-funded, three-day drunk. Actually, it didn't last three full days. We arrived at the conference location at noon on Wednesday and departed at noon on Friday.

The first of these I ever attended was during my first year of employment, 1971. Barry and I had been hired the same day, but we were sent to different locations. His duty station was a two-man office that served three counties in the western part of the state. His officemate was an experienced officer named Billy Hart. So the first night of our first conference, Billy and Barry went out on the town. We were headquartered in a large hotel, and the next morning, I went to the hotel restaurant for breakfast. There, I encountered Billy and Barry sitting on opposite sides of a booth.

Billy always had this poop-eating grin on his face, so I really didn't notice anything unusual about him. Barry, on the other hand, was sitting as still as a statue. He did not appear to be breathing, and I swear that if his mouth had been hanging open, I would have sworn he was dead and had just been propped up there for the sake of appearances. Still grinning like a jackass eating briars, Billy asked, "Do you know where our state car is?" I thought he was going to tell me something funny, like, maybe, that it had been impounded or that they had gotten it stuck in a ditch while under the influence. So I said, "Where?" Never changing his expression, Billy replied, "That's what I'm asking: do you know where it is? Because we sure as hell don't."

At the 1973 conference, I had an amusing episode with a state car myself. A secretary from another office where I had worked was in town visiting family and needed a ride from the conference hotel to her brother's residence. I borrowed a car from another officer and offered to drive her there. Now, I'm not going to tell you I wasn't planning a little extracurricular activity along the way. Maybe I was, and maybe I wasn't; you decide.

Anyway, I knew nothing at all about this town. To make matters worse, I was several sheets to the wind. So I'm driving in the inside lane of this heavily -traveled fourlane road – no idea where the hell I am – when Jackie says, "Turn left here. No, no; turn NOW!" Don't let this come as a revelation, but men and women are different. When someone tells a man to turn, he interprets that as "TURN NOW, DAMMIT!" So I did. Well, Jackie actually meant at the next street. The upshot was that I wound up with a state car stuck in a grassy median and drunk as Cooter Brown. I was already formulating a story in my mind to explain how the car ran off the road. I thought about puncturing one of the tires and claiming it had blown out, but I remembered how poor our agency was and how hard it was to get supplies like tires. I finally decided I would just tell the truth: Jackie had gotten mad and grabbed the wheel. Thankfully, I was able to rock the vehicle back and forth and free it, so we never had to face that.

One of our conferences was held in conjunction with a gathering of agencies from several southern states. Our state was the host, and some of us younger officers were recruited to serve as bartenders in the hospitality room. We actually had two adjoining rooms connected by a Dutch door—you know, the kind where you can open the top portion while the bottom remains closed. In one of these rooms were the bartenders (us) and the booze while in the other room were the drunks—er, guests! I don't recall who was in charge of this part of the conference, but whoever it was had told us that if we wanted to serve a particular guest a "special" (translation: strong) drink to hold the glass out of sight while filling it so the other drinkers wouldn't see you and feel like they were being shortchanged.

My boss Frank Sharp liked to drink and made no secret of the fact that he imbibed every night. I had been out drinking with Frank before, and I knew that he preferred straight bourbon. Oh, he would drop an ice cube or two into his glass to make it look like he had bourbon and water, but I knew better. So, as duly instructed, I held his glass out of sight behind the bottom portion of the door and filled it up with just bourbon. The whiskey was room temperature, so I added a couple of ice cubes. In a few minutes, Frank was back for another drink. He was grinning like a possum, and his eyes were glazed over. He handed me his glass and slurred, "I'll tell you one thing: if you ever stop working for the parole board, you'll make a hell of a bartender."

Frank pulled a stunt at one of our conferences that was the stuff legends are made of. The conference was always held in October, and fall temperatures in the south, believe it or not, can get a little chilly. You will meet Ronnie Taylor in the next couple of paragraphs, but for now, suffice it to say that he was very prim and proper. Everything was according to Hoyle, no foolishness allowed. Imagine his surprise, then, when he was awakened in the early morning hours by someone knocking frantically on the door of his motel room. As he later told it, Ronnie opened the door, when what to his wondering eyes should appear but a shivering Frank Sharp—totally naked.

Overcoming his shock, Ronnie brought Frank into his room, got him a blanket, and was able to get the front desk to send someone to let Frank into his own room. That's right—he was locked out. Now, here's his story. Decide for yourself whether you believe it. Frank claimed that he always slept in the buff (something I really didn't want to know). He said he was awakened by a knock at his room door and that he answered the door in his birthday suit. Hmm…not something I would have done. Then, from the gospel according to Frank, and for reasons known only to him, he stepped out onto the balcony naked as the day he was born, whereupon his door slammed shut and locked behind him. Yeah, I know: I thought it was a little weak myself, but whatever.

In the mid-seventies, the parole board decided that we should become RP (real police), complete with guns (which we had to furnish) and badges. In order to carry weapons, we had to be certified by the Peace Officers Standards and Training Commission. This certification normally required attendance at a six-week police academy; however, since we had all been working in the law enforcement field for a number of years, we were given a one-week crash course, then "grandfathered."

One day of that week was dedicated to learning basic and advanced first aid, which was taught by representatives of the Red Cross. Among other skills, we had to learn to perform cardiopulmonary resuscitation (CPR). The "victim" on whom you practice is a rubber dummy with a head and a torso, but no arms or legs. Two trainees were assigned to each dummy, one to provide chest compressions while the other did rescue breathing. The training dummy has a large balloon in its chest cavity, which breathing inflates. To be sure that you have the head positioned so that air can get to the lungs, you blow into the dummy's mouth then place your ear beside the mouth to listen for escaping air.

Well, after we paired off, there were three of us left. There was Ronnie Taylor, Ward Gordon, and me. Taylor and Gordon were supervisors from our central office, and two more different personalities could not be imagined. Ronnie was very serious, while Ward had a dry—and unpredictable—sense of humor.

Ward decided that he would be the first to do the breathing, so he blew a mighty breath into the dummy and placed his ear in the proper position to listen for the return air. Now, to appreciate this story, you must remember that these dummies consisted of a head and torso only—no limbs. So anyway, Ronnie and I were playing this straight, as if we were really trying to save this poor schmuck's life. Ward put his ear by the dummy's mouth and said, "What?" Then he looked at Ronnie and me, very seriously, and said, "He says he can't feel his legs." Caught us totally flat-footed.

Like I said, Ronnie Taylor was a very uptight, straitlaced person. Ronnie's full name was Benjamin Ronald Taylor, and like me, he used his first name and middle initial in his signature and official correspondence. Ronnie had a job with the parole board, which required him to interact with his counterparts in other paroling authority offices around the country, and I suppose he must have decided that *Ronnie* was too casual a name for someone in his position.

At any rate, he began answering telephone calls with "This is Benjamin R. Taylor." Fortunately, although Ronnie occupied a much loftier position than my own, I had known him for several years and knew that I could get by with what I did next. I had to call him one day, and he answered with his stuffy "This is Benjamin R. Taylor" shtick. I said, "Ronnie, you are one pompous ass!" Needless to say, he was a bit taken aback, but he did chuckle before replying, "What do you mean?" I said, "Who the hell answers the phone with their full name? Jeez, you ain't the president. Get over yourself." Ronnie laughed, but he did change his phone greeting.

Ronnie's was not the only bizarre telephone greeting at our central office. In the eighties, the agency decided that they needed an automated answering telephone system. You know the type: you get a recording that wastes a lot of your time and says virtually nothing of any use. Well, the first time I called the central office and encountered the recording, here's what it said: "You have reached the State Board of Pardons and Paroles. Our office is located at ________, and our business hours are eight a.m. to five p.m. Monday through Friday." So far pretty standard, right? But then, this disembodied voice continued—and I'm not making this up—"If you wish to speak to a person, press zero." Umm, you know, I really didn't call just to listen to the recording.

Of course, Ronnie Taylor was not the only by-the-book person in the department. When I began working for the parole board, the executive director was a late-sixties man by the name of J. B. Stanley. Mr. Stanley always stood ramrod straight, and he had piercing eyes that could freeze you in your tracks. We called him, affectionately (somewhat), the Hawk.

Mr. Stanley was one of the original fifteen parole officers hired when the parole board was created in 1937. As executive director, he was a real penny pincher. Of course, this was necessary to a degree, as our agency was perennially underfunded. When we had cars, they were likely to be turn-ins from other departments, some with two hundred thousand miles on them. Mr. Stanley was a micromanager when it came to the budget, and any expenditure had to be personally approved by him. One year, we were so strapped for cash that he instructed those of us with state vehicles to take them to our local state trooper post to have the antifreeze changed then report the cost to him. Accordingly, I dutifully drove my worn-out Ford to a nearby trooper station to get the work performed.

Now, when this car was assigned to me, it was wearing three radial tires and one bias-ply—not a recommended combination. In addition, two of the tires were showing cord. Very dangerous. So while I was at the state trooper post, I decided to, ahem, beg. I showed my car to the post commander, a blustering Yankee major, and asked (pleaded) for some tires they might have removed from their own cars and were planning to discard.

Boy, did I unleash a rant! This major went on a tirade that would have made a sailor blush. The nicest thing he said began with "That damned parole board." The whole time, I was nodding my head vigorously—in agreement. Hey, sometimes you gotta do what you gotta do to get things done. Anyway, after he had vented his spleen, this major turned to one of his garage workers and said, "Pick him out some of the best takeoffs and mount them on this rag." The cost was $2.50 each, to cover their expenses for mounting and balancing.

When I got back to my office, I called Mr. Stanley. The conversation went like this: "Mr. Stanley, this is Glenn Melton. I wanted to advise you that I had the antifreeze in my car changed today. And by the way, while I was there, I got four new tires." Well, I could have heard the old man from six blocks away without a telephone. Assuming that I had obligated the department to pay retail price for some new rubber, he almost had an apoplexy. "You did what?" I quickly added, "They only cost me $2.50 each." Without missing a beat, Mr. Stanley replied, "Can you get any more?" I said, "Sir, I had to sell my soul and promise my firstborn just to get four. However, if you like, I'll give you the name of the post commander, and you can call him. He seems to really like our agency."

Josh Stanford was a nice guy. Boring as hell, but nice. He was one of these people to whom you didn't dare say, "How are you?" Because he'd tell you, and in graphic detail. In fairness, Josh did have some medical problems, one of which was duodenal ulcers. Finally, he had no choice but to undergo surgery, during which his doctor split him open like a watermelon, from his sternum down to, um, let's just say the bottom of his abdomen. Now, if you've ever been cut like that or if you know someone who has, you know that stitches alone won't hold the incision together. After sewing Josh up, the surgeons had clamped his torso together in several places with large metal staples.

One day, months after his recovery, Josh appeared in the office, his normal hang-dog countenance worse than usual. I asked him what his problem was, and he said, "You know that ulcer surgery I had? Well, they think they may have left one of those staples inside me. If so, they're gonna have to cut me open again." I really liked Josh, but this was just too good to pass up. I said, "Josh, Josh, Josh. Don't you know all those doctors ever want to do is cut? Why, hell, man, there's no need to cut you open to get that staple out." Josh looked at me very seriously and said, "Really?" I replied, "Why, yes. We'll just go down to Sadler Steel [this was a large scrap metal company], and I'll take that big old electromagnet they use to lift cars, put it against your stomach, and pull it down real quick, which will jerk that staple right out of your ass." By this time, we had attracted some other officers, and of course, they all laughed uproariously. All except Josh, that is. He got this sad look on his face and said, "That's not funny." Which, of course, just made it that much funnier.

It's too bad the US Mint doesn't make currency with little handles on it. If they had, Josh might have been able to hold on to some of his. As it was, if Josh saw something he wanted, he bought it, whether he could afford it or not. His purchases included a huge four-bedroom house—and he and his wife didn't even have kids at the time. In addition, he never saw a gun he didn't love. Now, that's kind of a hazard in the law enforcement profession. Some people collect stamps or coins; cops like guns. Josh must have owned thirty or forty of them. If he saw one that caught his fancy, he just pulled out the old charge card and added to his arsenal. In addition, he bought his clothes at the most exclusive men's shop in town, explaining that he liked to look successful.

I had no idea how Josh could afford all these luxuries, as I knew that he made less than I did and his wife had a modest-paying state job. I would never have asked him how he accomplished his financial finagling, however. For one thing, I was raised to believe that nosy questions constituted bad manners, and furthermore, it was really none of my business.

One day, though, completely unbidden, Josh decided to reveal the secret behind his financial acumen. Several of us were seated around a table in the courthouse snack bar when, completely unrelated to anything we had been discussing, Josh took a paper napkin and began writing on it. He drew a vertical line down the center of the napkin, and on the left side of the line he listed his and his wife's net monthly income. As I surmised, together they made less than my wife and I did. Then, to the right of the line, he began listing his monthly debts. To this day, I've never seen anything quite like it.

When he had finished enumerating his required monthly payments, he added the column. It was clear that his income was exceeded—rather significantly, I might add—by his outgo. I was stunned. Manners be damned, I had to know how he was pulling this off, so I asked him. He gave me a look that implied that he was about to impart to me some major secret of financial legerdemain, then he replied, without a hint of irony, "Good credit." Dan Packer was seated to my right, and I looked at him in open-mouthed astonishment. He was the first to laugh, then we all just fell apart. The look on Josh's face made it clear that he believed he had offered a perfectly logical explanation to what was clearly an impossible situation and had no clue as to why we were laughing.

Like I said, Josh always had this hang-dog look on his face. Between his appearance and the fact that questions about his health always elicited a response beginning with "Oohhh," I had christened him—behind his back, of course—a basset hound. One morning, during our pre-work coffee and gab session, our boss Dave Drollet brought a top from a box that had contained a pair of Hush Puppies boots. For those who never knew or don't remember, their print ads always included a picture of a basset hound. Drollet never said a word; he just pulled out the box top. Cracked us up. Drollet was dry and droll, but occasionally he could come up with a good funny.

Another morning, while we were all drinking coffee, he said, "You know, I read this interesting article in a men's magazine. It seems that while taking their morning shower, about half of men play with themselves, while the other half sing. And what's really interesting is that those who sing almost all sing the same song." Then he fixed me with his normal squinting gaze and asked, "Do you know what the song is?" Well, I caught it right away, so I said, "Yes, I know." He then looked at the officer-in-charge, Frank Sharp, who also replied in the affirmative. There was a pregnant pause, then Dan Packer said, "Well, I don't know." We didn't let him live that one down for a while.

The office where I began my career as a probation and parole officer was located in the extreme southern part of the state. One of my coworkers was a young guy by the name of John Roy Ledford III. It was the consensus of opinion in the office that Ledford had been raised so far back in the sticks that his family had had to import sunshine. He spoke very slowly, with a pronounced Southern drawl. We joked that when he had to testify in court, you could catch a quick nap while he gave his name. It went like this: "Mah name is Johhhn…Royyy…Ledford…the Third." Since he always used *the third*, we decided to assign him a nickname. We called him Turd.

Now, Turd had taken a couple of courses in karate and considered himself an undiscovered Bruce Lee. He was shorter than me, and one of his favorite things to do, especially when he wanted to impress somebody, was to do a karate kick toward my face, his foot stopping only inches from my chin. I had grown weary of this little charade, so the next time he tried it—which was in our outer office, in full view of our secretaries—I made a swift move underneath his foot and grasped him firmly by his family jewels. Until then, I had no idea he could hold his foot in the air that long. By now, we were very close. It looked like we were about to dance a tango. I whispered in his ear, "You do that again, and I swear I'll yank 'em off. Got it?" I really don't think Turd could have uttered a word at that moment, but he nodded weakly, so I released him. Sometime later, he told me, "Ah never knew that wuz pissin' yew off." I replied, "You do now."

Turd was not what you would call handsome. The word I heard most of the women apply to him was *cute.* He was about five nine with a stylish mod haircut and a little mustache, and he definitely considered himself a lady killer. One of his female clients was a nasty drunk named Eve. I say nasty because she always came to our office reeking of alcohol. On top of that, she was hygienically challenged. But she made no secret of the fact that she had the hots for Turd.

One day, Turd and I were standing in the outer office when Eve came in. She gave Turd what I am sure she thought was a seductive smile and said, "I need to see you—alone!" I had a pretty good idea what was coming; Turd obviously did not. He and Eve went to his office and closed the door. Our office doors opened inward, so I grabbed Turd's door handle and placed my foot against the door jamb. I said to the secretaries, "Watch this."

I had no sooner gotten the words out of my mouth when I heard Turd yell, "WHOA! GET YOUR HANDS OFF ME, WOMAN!" He yanked on his door a couple of times, still yelling at Eve to leave him alone. Finally, I let him out. The secretaries were about to fall out of their chairs. Turd, on the other hand, was not a happy camper. Hey, I figured a karate expert could handle a drunken slut, you know?

If, in your mind's eye, Eve is stereotypical of female parolees and probationers, be advised that not all of them are so skanky. Even though a few are attractive, a law enforcement officer—at least, one who thinks with the big head—learns early in his career that having a personal relationship with a client or an arrestee is stupid. In the first place, it's unethical and in complete violation of the regulations of every law enforcement agency of my acquaintance. However, if one is not burdened with a moral code and really doesn't mind losing his job, there is one additional thing to consider before, ahem, *doing* it, and that is a law which prohibits such conduct on the grounds that a person who is in a custodial relationship may not feel free to refuse advances from an officer. I understood these prohibitions thoroughly and never violated them; still, there was one time when I gave it serious consideration.

Terry Montgomery was one of the cutest little girls I had ever seen. She was about 5 feet three inches, slim, and clearly middle class or above. She had just been paroled from the state penitentiary for women and was reporting to our office in search of her assigned parole officer, Dan Packer. Now, at the time, I was about thirty-two years old and not bad looking. No brag, just fact.

The first time I laid eyes on Terry—and that was all I ever laid on her—the glance that passed between us was hot enough to make the great Chicago fire look insignificant. To put it bluntly, we wanted each other, and it showed. When she left Packer's office, I asked him about her. It seems that she had just finished serving part of a prison sentence for the offense of murder. The victim of her crime was her boyfriend, who, according to her testimony, had been abusing her. So, from across a twenty-foot room, she shot him. Now, get this: she said she only intended to scare him, so she turned her head away before firing the fatal shot. Nevertheless, the bullet struck him in the heart, causing his immediate demise. Oops. End of attraction. I mean, hell, I couldn't shoot that well facing the target with both eyes open wide. She most assuredly was someone you would not have wanted to make mad.

One office where I was stationed as a parole and probation officer had a female supervisor by the name of Karen Fluker. Karen was plain. *Very* plain. And I say that not to be mean; on the contrary, I'm being charitable. How plain was she, you ask (I knew you wanted to know)? Let's put it this way: If I were compiling a dictionary, I would leave out the definition of the word and put her picture in its place. Seen a few like that? Thought so.

Well, anyway, one day I was summoned to appear in court in a small town in the southern part of the state to testify in a probation revocation hearing. I really didn't want to go, as the round trip alone would take four hours, effectively consuming my day. Still, I knew that the defense lawyer was banking on my not showing, and without corroborating testimony, the charges of probation violation would be dismissed. I wasn't about to let that happen. At the time, I did not have a state car assigned to me. I mentioned earlier in this chapter that our vehicles were refugees from a junkyard, and Karen's was no exception. It was an old Dodge Diplomat that the state motor pool had worn out before passing it on to us. Still, it was the best vehicle available, so I used it to go to the hearing. The defense lawyer was surprised to see me there and decided to have the probationer plead guilty to the charge—good move, as I had enough evidence to crucify his client.

Upon my return to my office, I handed Plain Karen her keys and said, "You need to have your car worked on. At eighty, the air conditioner stops blowing [true]." Karen bristled, "What do you mean driving my car eighty miles per hour?" I smiled sweetly while considering how much time I might get for killing her and replied, "Mrs. Fluker, allow me to enlighten you, if I may. You see, that vehicle belongs to the parole board, which makes it as much mine as yours. And the reason I drove it eighty is that the damn thing wouldn't go any faster [true again]."

One day I was in my office when I heard Karen in the outer office extemporizing to the secretaries. A national chain drive-in restaurant—the retro fifties kind, where the car hops roller-skate to your car with your order—had opened a location in our town. The secretaries were all in their twenties and thirties, so they had never seen a drive-in restaurant. Karen was telling them how there had been a number of these places in our city during the fifties and early sixties. Now, to make this funny, you need to know that I was actually a couple of years older than Karen.

The little devil on my shoulder said, "Hey, go out there and see if she'll feed you a straight line. She probably won't, but it's worth a try." So I walked out to the secretarial area and sidled up beside Karen. And wonder of wonders, she did it. She looked at me and said, "You remember all the drive-ins we had in the fifties, don't you?" I could barely contain my glee as I replied, "No, Karen, that was *way* before my time." No sense of humor. Shame.

When I was a police officer, many of us had nicknames. Mine was Fido, and I came by it quite innocently. One night, I was stopped in a parking lot writing a report when a citizen approached my patrol car and informed me that someone had hanged a dog in a nearby park. I thought maybe this guy was putting me on, but of course, I was obligated to check it out. Sure enough, in the back of the park, some heartless creep had hanged a poor little dog on the fence surrounding a softball field. I made a report, and at the end of my shift, I took it and the other reports I had written that evening and was logging them in on the police blotter at the record room when I got stumped. For each report, there was a blank on the blotter labeled Victim. A sergeant I knew well was standing beside me, and I said, "Hey, Sarge, did you hear that call I had tonight? The one about the dog?" He said yes, so I asked him, "What do I put for victim? I don't know the dog's name." Now, in fairness, we both knew that the state was recorded as the victim in a case like this, but he saw the humor in the situation and replied, "Put Fido," which I did. Beside Fido, the good sergeant wrote "hung dog."

When I reported for duty the next evening, I was met by a sergeant (not the same one), who proceeded to chew my ass out to a fare-thee-well. Not long after that, I had a similar encounter with his boss, the lieutenant. Finally, I was summoned to meet the watch commander, a captain, at headquarters. When I entered the room, I told him, "If you're here to chew my ass out, you're too damn late. Sarge got the left cheek, and the lieutenant got what was left." The captain was an easy-going sort, and he just laughed and said, "Do you know why we made such a big issue of this?" When I said no, he told me that the local newspaper had access to the police blotter and that if they saw anything thereon that piqued their interest, they might write a story about it. Apparently they were considering a story about Fido Hung Dog when somebody at the department intervened. From that day forward I was Fido.

One of my supervisors at the police department was a wiry little sergeant named Rod Delaney. Rod was a smart guy, but he was about as personable as a pit bull. He had a very high opinion of himself and his abilities, so it was always fun to embarrass him or bring him down a notch.

On one such occasion, I had stopped for my thirty-minute meal break at a fast-food restaurant. Upon returning to my patrol car, I discovered that the battery was dead, so I called on my walkie-talkie for a unit with jumper cables to come jump me off. Sergeant Delaney apparently had nothing to do, so he came also. Now, visualize the scene, if you will: there are three police cars pulled up at this restaurant. Make you think something serious is happening, wouldn't it? Well, about this time, a lady pulled up to the restaurant in a small hatchback automobile. Apparently the presence of all the police cars distracted her because as she exited her car and closed the door, she got a sick look on her face and said, "Oh my god, I just locked my keys in my car."

Wanting to play the hero, Sergeant Delaney puffed out his little chest and said, "I'll take care of this." Whereupon he retrieved from his vehicle a slim jim, a thin flat metal bar capable—in trained hands—of being inserted into the window channel of a vehicle door and opening the lock. Unfortunately, it quickly became apparent that Sergeant Delaney was not very skillful with his toy.

While he was engaged in on-the-job training with his slim jim, I walked around the car to see if any of the other doors might be open. This vehicle did not have electric locks, so each door had to be locked individually. And would you believe my luck? The rear hatch was unlocked. But I didn't tell anybody. Instead, I squatted down and pretended to give a mighty pull on the hatch while grunting loudly. "Miraculously," I got the hatch open! As I am not particularly muscular, everybody present looked at me curiously. I used the line from *Superman II*, where Superman thrashes a bully who had beat him up when he temporarily gave up his superpowers: "I've been, um, working out." The driver was profoundly grateful, and the sergeant had egg on his face. A twofer. What a day!

Sergeant Delaney's biggest problem was that he took life way too seriously. As you may have surmised by now, I don't. Never have. Hey, you're not getting out of this life alive, so why not have some fun while you're here?

It was midnight on a warm summer night, and I had just come on duty when I was dispatched to the scene of a murder-suicide. I arrived at a lower-income apartment complex to find several people standing around a man lying motionless on his back on the ground. Nearby was a .32 caliber revolver with which he had shot himself in the head. A quick examination revealed that he had no vital signs, and I knew that the paramedics were en route, so I asked where the murder victim was. I was directed to an upper level apartment in which a found a heavyset woman with a rag being held against her head by her adult son. There was a lot of blood, but the victim was conscious and talking. I learned from her relatives that the shooter was a jilted boyfriend who, after shooting her in the head, had run outside and killed himself. Fortunately for this woman, the shot to her head had missed both her brain and her optic nerve. The only lasting damage it caused her was that it destroyed a couple of her sinuses. No more sinus headaches for her!

Upon arrival of detectives from our violent crimes unit, I turned the investigation over to them and got back in service. After things had quieted down, I checked out by radio at an all-night cafe for some breakfast. I was about to dig into a plate of scrambled eggs with ketchup on them (hey, I like ketchup on eggs, okay?) when I was joined by Sergeant Delaney. Looking at my delicacy, he got a sort of nauseated look on his face and said, "You got that murder-suicide call earlier, didn't you?" Without looking up from my meal, I replied, "Yep." Delaney asked, "Both of them head shots, right?" I replied, "Mm hm." Looking a little incredulous, he said, "You're a sick puppy!" I replied, "Nope. *Hungry* puppy. Big difference." I believe he was truly shaken.

Speaking of eating, cops are frequently parodied as doughnut hounds. True? I can speak only for myself, but I was fond of snacking, and my waistline showed it. We rotated shifts every three months, and I was particularly susceptible to the munchies when I was assigned to first watch, which began at midnight.

On one of the beats I patrolled, there was a location of a well-known doughnut chain. You might not know this, but after doughnuts have sat in the case for a while, the store will throw them out, considering them too stale for consumption. Well, I knew exactly when this particular shop rotated their doughnuts, and I was there to scoop up the rejects, unless I was on a call at the time. I had a secret code that I would broadcast over the radio, which was the signal to my squad mates to converge at a predetermined location and pig out (damn, shouldn't have said *pig*).

On another of my beats was a little hole-in-the-wall shop modestly named the Best Doughnuts. The owner was the only employee, and I knew his schedule precisely. He would arrive at the shop at four in the morning to begin cooking. This place was located in a very high crime rate area of the city, so I would make several passes by his shop between then and daybreak, shining my spotlight through the takeout window on each trip to let him know I was there. The minute the doughnuts were ready, I would stop and order some. One morning, the owner said, "Thank you for keeping such a close watch on me during the wee hours. Makes me feel safe." I smiled and said, "You, hell! I'm checking to see when the doughnuts are ready." Which wasn't far off the truth.

By the time doughnut-devouring time rolled around, the city was usually pretty quiet, so I could enjoy my delicacies in peace. However, there was one notable exception. I had decided to vary my wee hours cuisine. I stopped at a convenience store, and after chatting up the clerk for a while, I bought a chocolate cake–type snack with a cream center and returned to my car. This little treat had apparently sat in the warm store too long, as it was soft and gooey. Just as I got my mouth stuffed with about half of it, the dispatcher called me. "One oh seven [my unit number], assist 109. He has a vehicle refusing to stop. It's a hearse." I damn near choked on my dessert trying to answer that one. "Mmph, mmph [swallow]…a WHAT?" The dispatcher responded, trying to suppress a laugh, "That's right, a hearse." So I boogey on over to where I assumed, from their reported direction of travel, the procession would be, intercepting the low-speed pursuit and blocking the hearse. Seems one of the embalmers had inhaled a little too much formaldehyde (or booze) and decided to take a joy ride. We arrested the driver and called the owner of the funeral home to come retrieve his vehicle. He arrived, none too happy about the situation, and fired the besotted driver on the spot. No sense of humor at all.

The police department where I worked did not place a lot of emphasis on physical fitness, and it showed in the, ahem, *size* of some of our officers. In addition to considering himself a paragon of virtue, Sergeant Delaney took great pride in staying in good shape. Of course, he wasn't married and was not in high demand by the ladies, so really, what else did he have to do? Anyway, after I had been working there for a couple of years, the department decided to invest in an obstacle course to whip us into fighting trim. Even though this was a pretty low-budget department, they did build a state-of-the-art facility—and it was a bear! Among its challenges was a wooden wall, approximately eight feet tall. The object of the game was to scale the wall, and Sergeant Delaney was there to show us (really, to show us up) how to do it. This wall was totally vertical and had no handholds. The result was that, in several attempts, I was not successful in getting over it.

Sergeant Delaney decided that he would embarrass me in front of my fellow officers. He got this smug look on his little face and said, "What if you are chasing somebody and he jumps over a wall? What are you going to do?" Oops. Never should have asked that one, Sarge. I replied, "Coincidentally, that happened to me two nights ago. I was in foot pursuit of a suspect in a residential neighborhood, and he went over a six-foot brick wall around someone's yard." Delaney was sure he had me by the short hairs now, so he folded his arms with obvious satisfaction and asked, "So what did you do?" I said, "Well, you know, I figured that the homeowners had not built a wall without putting a gate in it. I found the gate, opened it, went in the yard, and apprehended the suspect." Gotcha!

Losing that little exercise in mental gymnastics must have flustered the good sergeant, because during his next demonstration of wall vaulting, he landed on his back, banging his head on the ground that had been only slightly cushioned with a layer of sawdust. He was taken to the local hospital to have his head x-rayed, and I was informed on reliable authority that the doctors found nothing (I can believe it).

Cops always like to know that their fellow officers have enough guts to stand beside them, no matter the situation. In fact, one of my first instructions to any rookie I had to train was "Whatever you do, don't ever run. If we are in a dangerous situation and it appears that I'm about to be killed, you'd better die with me. Run, and you'll die with my bullet in your back. Got it?" A couple of them looked at me as if trying to gauge whether I was serious or not. Was I? I'll never tell. But I never had one run.

Betty Wiggins was the smallest police officer I have ever seen, before or since. She was five feet tall and weighed maybe ninety pounds dripping wet and wearing all her gear. I first met Betty during her training at the police academy, when I was asked to help some of the less-experienced newbies with firearms training. Betty did fairly well shooting a pistol, so I handed her a twelve-gauge shotgun to try. Any of you who has ever fired a shotgun knows that you don't stand with both feet beside each other. Instead, you place one foot farther back, in an athletic stance, to help maintain your balance, as a shotgun has a significant amount of recoil. Well, Betty put her feet in exactly the wrong position. I started to correct her; then, recalling the maxim about experience being the best teacher, I thought—nah. Sure enough, the first shot she fired knocked her flat on her butt. But it didn't happen again. Mission accomplished.

Betty graduated from the academy—and was assigned to my squad! Now, this scared the hell out of me. I just knew that her size would make her useless as a backup in a situation involving violence. She had been on the job about a month when my theory was put to the test.

I was dispatched to the scene of a fight between women, and Betty was sent to assist. I quickly determined that one of the combatants was the instigator and would have to be arrested. Two problems: she was highly intoxicated, and she was big, about five nine and two hundred pounds. It was clear from her reaction to being told she was under arrest that she had no intention of going quietly. I grabbed her left wrist and was in the process of applying handcuffs to it when my peripheral vision picked up her right hand being formed into a fist and drawn back. I braced for impact, realizing that this woman's size and street experience would make her a formidable opponent. But lo and behold, she didn't hit me. I looked up and saw that little Betty, who was quiet and mild-mannered, had very gently placed her hand on this perpetrator's throat and almost whispered, "Stop." And she did! Of course, I was happy not to have had to fight this wild woman. Still, I considered her response just a lucky fluke.

About a week later, I was dispatched to a domestic disturbance involving a married couple. Again, Betty was sent to back me up. Well, the same thing happened. I went to arrest Bubba, and he drew back as if to fight. Again, gentle little Betty placed her hand very lightly on the guy's throat and said, "Stop." Worked again. In this situation, I decided the guy had better sense than to attack a small female officer, figuring I would probably kill him if he tried. At any rate, these two incidents had a profound effect on my opinion of Betty's value. On later occasions, when I was dispatched on a dangerous call and knew that I would be getting backup, I would radio, "Umm, could you, umm, send 110 [her unit number]?" Hey, I might have been a chauvinist, but I wasn't a *dumb* chauvinist.

It will probably come as no surprise to learn that not all new hires become effective police officers. Some wash out in the academy, which is what should have happened to Linda Larson. Her class was receiving training on proper handcuffing procedure. Linda had a "rowdy suspect" (another trainee) pinned against her vehicle and was to apply cuffs to him. Instead, she handcuffed her own wrists. *Both* of her own wrists. To make this almost unbelievable, you have to know that she was black—and the suspect was white! Hmm…looks like she could have seen the difference.

For reasons I could not comprehend, Linda graduated and was assigned to street patrol. Almost immediately, I could tell that she was in way over her head. For example, I was assigned to take several of the rookies and work escort for the downtown Christmas parade. We all parked our vehicles facing in the direction that the parade was to go so that we would be ready to escort when they were ready to commence. All except Linda, that is. She parked facing the wrong way. I won't repeat what I told her, but I think that when I was through, she clearly understood that my opinion of her was not terribly high.

On another occasion, our dispatcher notified Linda by radio to telephone the 911 center. Sometimes there were things that dispatch did not want everybody with a police scanner to hear. For example, if dispatch advises the possible location of a fugitive and he happens to have a scanner, he's likely to boogey. Now, this was in the days before cellular phones had been invented, so Linda replied, "Headquarters, I do not have a phone in this car." There was a lengthy pause (during which, I'm sure, all the dispatchers were laughing too hard to respond). Finally one of them said, "Umm, you do know what a pay phone is, don't you?" Linda was fired (thank you, Jesus) not long after that debacle.

I talk more about rookies in another chapter, but as a training officer, I frequently had one riding with me. It was my job to teach him or her how to apply the lessons learned in the police academy to real police work. When things were slow, I sometimes interspersed a little extracurricular activity to relieve the boredom.

As I mentioned in another chapter, most of us found it necessary, when working first watch (midnight to 8:00 a.m.), to sneak off somewhere for a little nap. One of the officers in my squad, Tyrone Jackson, apparently thought he should get his whole night's sleep while on duty. After things quieted down, usually around 2:00 a.m., you couldn't find him anywhere.

Quite by accident, I had stumbled onto the location of his hidey hole. It was down a little pig trail and right beside a seldom-used railroad track. About three o'clock one morning, things were deathly quiet, and my rookie and I were trying manfully to stay awake. I looked at him and said, "Hey, you want to have some fun?" Naturally, he was game, so I turned my car lights off, and we eased quietly up behind Tyrone's car. Sure enough, his head was thrown back on the headrest. He was clearly deep in dreamland. I adjusted my vehicle-mounted spotlight so that when I turned it on, it would be shining directly in his mirror. Then, I looked at my rookie with a mischievous grin and counted, "One…two…three!" Simultaneously, I flipped on my spotlight and sat down on the air horn built into my vehicle's siren system. Needless to say, Tyrone awoke with a start. He almost hurt himself trying to get his car started, assuming from the light and the horn, which I was blowing unmercifully, that he had accidentally parked on the tracks! Once he realized he had been had, Tyrone was not amused; however, I did hear that he never slept well on duty again.

Lest by now you have come to the conclusion that I never got the short end of the joke, allow me to disabuse you of that notion. As a police officer, I worked in a fairly large city whose per capita income was somewhat low by regional standards. The police department's budget, of course, came from city taxes collected. As a result, some of our equipment was low-budget. Oh, hell, let's tell it like it was: it was crap. When I first arrived, the agency was just beginning to purchase take-home patrol cars for its officers. As a result, most of us had to check a vehicle out of the department motor pool before beginning our shift. There was not an overabundance of cars, so most of them served all three shifts, meaning they ran twenty-four hours a day, seven days a week.

Now, the cars were wired so that the revolving blue light on the roof, which we referred to as the bubble gum machine, would work with the car's ignition off. The siren, however, would not operate unless the vehicle was running. It was not uncommon to get into your car and switch on the ignition, only to have the siren start screaming. This wasn't so bad on second and third shifts, but our first watch began at midnight, and police headquarters was located right next to a residential area. I'm sure the residents who were awakened because of somebody's idea of a prank saw the humor in the situation (not!).

After checking out your unit and before proceeding to your assigned beat (patrol area), there were two tasks you needed to complete. The first was to look the car over and duly note any damage, including missing hubcaps, so that you would not be held responsible for the problem later. Then it was recommended that you check the rear seat area for any contraband that a prisoner might have disposed of while being transported to the jail. The officer performing the arrest should have looked here after placing the offender in jail; however, some did not. And to be honest, if the arresting officer performed a proper search at the time of arrest, there should not have been any contraband for the prisoner to get rid of anyway.

Well, one night I had obtained my vehicle and was examining the rear seat area when I found—a pistol! Now, this made my blood run cold because even though it turned out to be a replica that could fire only blanks, it could just as easily have been a real gun. Had it been real and had the offender been desperate enough, the officer might have lost his life. Even if this arrestee did not shoot him, the next person placed in that seat, finding a weapon readily available, might have. I was flabbergasted.

I confiscated the pistol; then I went back into headquarters to see who had driven this unit before me. I discovered it was a good young officer named Chuck Crater. Chuck and I had graduated from the police academy in the same class; however, he was assigned to a different shift than I was. The following night, I came in early so that I could speak with Chuck as he was getting off duty. When I showed him this pistol and explained to him how I had come into possession of it, he literally got weak in the knees and had to sit down. I said, "You know, Chuck, if this gun was real, it might have been used to blow your head off. Conversely, had I not spotted it, it could have been used on me." Chuck was mortified by his oversight and apologized profusely. I believed he had learned a very important lesson, so I never reported the incident to a supervisor.

Police officers are known for putting each other on the spot. Playfully, of course. One night I was dispatched to the scene of a domestic disturbance. As I mentioned in another chapter, domestics are the most dangerous calls cops respond to, accounting for more officer deaths than any other type of situation, so another unit was sent to back me up. Ernie Brown was a veteran officer, and to understand the gist of this story, you have to know that he was black. The sheriff's department in our town had very little to do, so one of their deputies decided to respond to this call as well.

Upon our arrival, I found a young woman hiding behind a vehicle. She told me that her husband had assaulted her but that she did not want to prosecute. She was clearly terrified of him. This was before passage of the federal law that now requires police to make an arrest if any injury is observed on a victim, and our agency had a policy not to arrest the perpetrator unless the victim agreed to testify against him in court. Still, we decided that we would talk to the husband and explain to him the inadvisability of beating on his wife. Our knock at the door was answered by a large, arrogant drunk. He was obviously aware that his wife would not prosecute him; I'm sure this was not the first time he had assaulted her. Our hands tied due to lack of a cooperating victim, we turned to leave, but big brave mouth could not leave well enough alone. He said, to our backs (of course), "Get off my porch, nigger."

I glanced at Ernie, who seemed to have taken the slur in stride. However, I decided that we had enough to charge this jerk with disorderly conduct, so I said, "Let's get him." The three of us charged through the screen door. I was leading the way, and I performed a flying tackle on the putz, winding up on the floor with his head in a choke hold. Ernie was applying handcuffs, but I kept hearing a noise: *whop, whop, whop.* I looked around in time to see the deputy, Butch Seay, striking the man on his shin bone with a heavy flashlight. I yelled, "Dammit, Seay, stop it! We have him in custody."

Ever known anybody who was just a glutton for punishment? Mr. Bigmouth decided he was still going to win, although he didn't have a card left to play. He refused several requests to get up and walk to my car. So Ernie got one leg and I took the other, and we dragged him to the vehicle. This was an older house, with five concrete steps leading to an elevated porch, and his head hit every step on the way down. No, it wasn't police brutality. We had to take him to jail, and we had given him several opportunities to stand up and walk.

Well, the next morning, we appeared in court to testify. The offender told his side of the story, then pointed at Ernie and said, "That black officer hit me with a stick, and I think he broke my leg." The judge looked at me, and I shrugged my shoulders and said, "Judge, I had him by the head. I don't know who—if anybody—hit him." I glanced sideways at Ernie, and his mouth was hanging open in absolute incredulity. After court, he said, "Uh huh, uh huh, I see how you are. Gonna let the black guy take the fall, weren't you? Leave your poor old fellow officer to twist in the wind. Uh huh." I nearly fell on the floor laughing.

The crowning glory of my practical joke repertoire also involved a rookie. Frequently, when we had a graduating class from the police academy, we would discover that a few of the graduates were a little, um, shall we say, skittish. We had a surefire cure for the real scaredy-cats. It worked like this.

On the east side of the city, really sort of out in the country, was a large park. Big Rock Park was probably two hundred acres. It was very rural, and going through it at night could be a little spooky. The public was banned from the park after dark, so when you got way back in the park, you and the wild critters, whose eyes you could clearly see, were theoretically the only living creatures there. It took a while to get through the park, so if you did run up on someone there and things got hairy, it was going to be a few minutes before backup could get to you.

We would attempt to select the most nervous rookie assigned to first watch. After we had selected our victim, his training officer would wait until things had settled down around 3:00 a.m. and then make the off-handed suggestion, "Hey, let's go ride through Big Rock Park." Now, remember, we did not have the sergeant in the trunk to monitor our movements. This gag would not be possible today because as soon as you left your beat (assigned territory), dispatch would know and would call to ask where you were going.

Anyway, as the training officer was driving through the park, he would "happen" on another patrol car, mysteriously abandoned. At this point, the training officer would look at the vehicle's number and say, "Hey, that's Vince's car. I wonder where he is." Then he would get out of the car, with the rookie following, and start calling, "Vince! Hey, Vince! Where are you?" Now, Vince had access to a very scary costume. I don't know if it belonged to a friend or whether he rented it, but it was a particularly realistic-looking (especially at night) gorilla suit. He would come running out of the woods like Bigfoot, screaming and growling, which generally had the effect of scaring the crap out of the rookie victim.

Well, enter that little old joker—me! I decided that the gag had become a little stale, so I resolved to liven it up a bit. My rookie was selected as the stooge, but I told him what was going to happen. I said, "When Vince comes running out of the woods, I want you to draw your weapon and fire a few rounds over his head."

The little play was going exactly per what Vince thought was the script. My rookie and I exited my car and began calling for Vince, who appeared right on cue, wailing like a banshee. Imagine his surprise when my rookie drew his service revolver and pointed it at him. I could see Vince's eyes—he was that close—and even in the dark, I could see the terror in them. He said, "Ahhh…shit…nooo," then turned and began running back toward the woods. My rookie aimed his gun well over Vince's head and fired—*boom…boom…boom.* The sound of gunfire so close to my ear partially deafened me temporarily, but I was still able to hear Vince screaming, "Eeaaghhh! Crazyassmotherfuckergonnakillme!" After the rookie and I were able to contain our laughter, I began calling for Vince, assuring him it was safe to come out. I don't know how far he ran into those woods, but I had to go to my car and get on the PA system before he heard me.

I had to confess to Vince that I had set him up. He did not see the humor in the situation, particularly because this was a borrowed or rented costume, and due to his, ahem, *apprehension* at the prospect of being shot, he had filled the bottom of the three-piece suit with feces. Lots of feces. How much? Ever had a colonoscopy? Neither have I, but I know several people who have. The day before the procedure, the patient has to drink enough laxative to kill seven goats and a mule. The goal is to get you so squeaky clean inside that nothing but water comes out of your rear end. Until Vince began removing his costume, I had no idea that the human body could hold that much crap. I have had some interesting experiences in my life, but standing in the middle of a deserted park in the middle of the night trying to clean poop out of a gorilla suit is near the top. It was clear that we needed some water, and we were miraculously able to find a storage shed that had been left unlocked (that's my story, and I'm sticking to it), from which we liberated a hose and began to wash the costume.

About this time, things went from bad to worse. Over my walkie-talkie, I heard a unit dispatched to Big Rock Park to investigate a report of shots fired. Now there we were, Vince and me, both off our beats, standing there washing doo-doo off a costume (and off Vince). I figured there was just one way to carry the gig off, so I grabbed the head portion of the costume and put it on. My rookie and I jumped in my car, and I told Vince, "You stay here and finish your laundry. I'll head off the cavalry." Just as the dispatched unit entered the park, I drove by them going out. Remember, I was wearing this gorilla head and driving my patrol car, and I flipped the other officer off and shouted, "Fuck you, pig!" I had no doubt he would figure out what was going on, which he must have done, as he checked back in on the radio and advised that the report of shots fired was unfounded.

I often wondered if our generation of miscreants had been the first to devise such devilish pranks. I still don't know, but I did come to the conclusion that the higher-ups probably were aware of our high jinks and had adopted a "no harm, no foul" policy. After all, as with any organization, happy campers do better work.

Actually, my avocation as a practical joker began way before I became a law enforcement officer. One of my career best occurred in high school. I was a high-ranking officer in the ROTC program there, and as such, I was expected to attend the military ball. Problem was, I had no idea how to dance. Well, a friend of mine confided that he also had two left feet and was taking dance lessons from a professional instructor, Bonnie Williams. My blessed mother did not want me to be embarrassed, so she paid for me to take lessons from this same woman.

Bonnie and her husband, Sid, were both instructors, and they taught ballroom dancing in their home. The house was a fifties ranch with one large rectangular room that served as a combination living-dining room. Theirs had been converted to a dance studio. There were wood floors, and one whole wall was covered with mirrors. After several weeks of instruction, I was ready. Bonnie casually inquired whether I might like for her and Sid to put on a dancing demonstration during the ball's intermission, to which I happily acquiesced.

The night of the ball, which was held in the school gym (does that bring back memories, or what?), came, and just before intermission, Bonnie and Sid arrived. The floor was cleared for them, but the announcer gave only their names, omitting the fact that they were dance instructors. As one lonely spotlight followed their smooth moves, they proceeded to dazzle the crowd with their expertise. Finally, the music stopped for a moment, and something happened that I will never forget.

Bonnie was a drop-dead gorgeous woman, maybe twenty-five, with a perfect figure, a dancer's taut legs, and flowing raven hair. I was seventeen, not much to look at, and being eaten alive by raging hormones. So of course, I was in love with her. Or maybe just in heat, I don't know. Anyway, that night she was wearing a short black cocktail dress and sequined gold pumps. May sound tacky now, but in 1963, it was haute couture.

She left Sid's side and, followed by the spotlight, half-walked, half-danced to within ten feet of where I sat on the front row of the bleachers. Then she raised her right hand, curled her index finger, and gave me the sexiest come-hither look I have ever seen, before or since. As the spotlight followed us, we danced a graceful, sensuous waltz, ending just in front of the bleachers. Before letting me go, Bonnie whispered something in my ear. I would love to say that it was "Smooth moves, you young stud," but as I recall, it was just a reminder of the date of my next lesson. I did a cock-of-the-walk stroll back to the bleachers where a bunch of glassy-eyed, slack-jawed cadets were sitting in envy so deep I could have cut it with a knife.

Now, up until that point, my popularity rating at school had been a little low, but suddenly I could not walk the halls without some horny guy grabbing me by the arm to ask about Bonnie. It was funny as hell because I always answered their questions honestly. Well, almost honestly. I told the truth, just not the whole truth. I told them how she and I would see each other about once a week, adding that she was a professional and that I paid for her services, how the room where we "did it" was covered with mirrors, and how her husband not only knew what we were doing but would often watch and demonstrate new "moves" for me. Damn near drove them crazy. That is, until the day my classmate—the one from whom I had learned about her—revealed the deception. That afternoon, I was walking to my car in the school parking lot when I encountered a few guys who were not too thrilled about being duped. But once I pointed out to them that I had not really lied, they eased up. A little.

I can honestly say that I have been a prankster for as long as I can remember. This tendency on my part almost drove my poor mother bonkers (another one of those psychological terms—see what I learned in six years of college? Impressive, isn't it?).

Mother was a registered nurse, in charge of a hall in a small hospital. We lived close by because she could not drive, and we had to be walking distance from her work. Since I was too young to be left at home alone, she had employed a domestic who cleaned the house and babysat me. Occasionally, this woman was unable to work, and on days like that, I was required to accompany my mother to the hospital for her eight-hour shift. I was allowed the run of the hospital, but I could not leave the building. Can you imagine how bored a seven-year-old can get locked inside a hospital for eight hours? I figured you could. Can you imagine the lengths to which that same child might go to relieve the monotony? I doubt it.

On one such occasion, I had gone to a floor other than the one on which my mother worked. And there—wonder of wonders—I discovered a high-backed wooden wheelchair (remember, this was the early fifties) like the one you see pictures of President Franklin Roosevelt riding in. Draped across the chair's arm was a white cotton hospital blanket. Well, of course, the frustrated actor who lived inside my little body got an idea. I got in the chair and covered my legs with the blanket. Man, did I look pitiful! It helps to remember that these were the days before development of the Salk polio vaccine, and it was not uncommon to see children who had been totally or partially paralyzed by this dreaded disease.

Anyway, I saw this couple coming my way, obviously there to visit someone. I twisted my arm and neck in my best imitation of a birth defect (yes, I know, it wasn't very nice, but hey, I was only seven); held my hand out, palm up; and made a sad little sound like, "Unhhh, oom, huhhh." Well, this kind couple was obviously moved by my plight, so they stopped and deposited a quarter in my hand. Again, let me remind you that this was maybe 1953, and at that time, I was getting a quarter a week allowance. This sounds like poverty wages today, but candy bars sold for a nickel, as did soft drinks, so it wasn't so bad.

After this couple left, I realized what a racket I had invented. I had received a whole quarter just for looking pathetic. Worked so well, I tried it on everybody who came by, with similar results. This charade continued for several minutes, during which I amassed what, to my childish mind, seemed like a fortune—probably a buck or so.

Now, in those days hospital floors were commercial linoleum, which was kept polished to a high gloss, and when nurses walked on them with their rubber-bottom shoes, they made a squeaking sound. Suddenly, I heard behind me the unmistakable sound of a nurse, and it was clear from the frequency of the squeaks that (1) she was approaching my location and (2) she was in one great big hurry. Before I could wheel my "crippled" body to safety, what seemed like the hand of God reached over the top of that wheelchair and literally pulled me straight up out of it. My mother got down to my level, looked me straight in the eyes, and said, between gritted teeth, "I am going to kill you. It may happen here, or I may wait until we're home, but I WILL kill you."

Bless her heart, she didn't get any relief even after I was grown. I earned my bachelor's degree at a small college in my hometown. In order to conserve money, I lived at home with my parents during those years. One night, I had been out doing some serious partying. I returned home in the wee hours of the morning so incapacitated that I could not get my key in the front door lock.

Well, I was expressing my anger toward this poor door in loud and profane terms. When I finally got inside, I pulled the door shut and locked it. I turned around and was confronted by my mother, all five feet three inches of her. She was wearing a robe and a disgusted look, and she had her arms folded across her chest. She said, "Humph, drunk again!" I smiled and replied, "Me too. Let's have a party."

I do believe, though, that the angriest I ever saw her was one day, years after I had reached adulthood, when I told her that she had taught me to lie. I mean, she was incensed. But hey, it was true. See, I grew up in a lower-middle-class neighborhood in the fifties. There were lots of other kids living nearby, including my next-door neighbor Joey Westin and the three Baxley brothers a few doors down. Geof was the eldest of the Baxleys, but he was a couple of years older than the rest of us and very mature for his age. Since he hung out with older kids, he was rarely involved in either our play or our squabbles. Mark was my age and a mean little snot, and his brother Donnie was a year or so younger.

Well, one day, all the rest had decided to pick on me (goat was a rotating position; one of them would be it the next day). I was handling the torment fairly well—that is, until they made the mistake of going on my front porch and stealing my prized bicycle. That was when the Verdigro hit the Mixmaster. I went into my apartment and retrieved a baseball bat, with which I began chasing them through the neighborhood, all the while calling them everything but children of God. My mother happened to be off work that day, and she calmly summoned me to the front door, whereupon she asked me what I had been calling the others. And I told her!

Now, you need to understand that my father was in the US Navy during World War II, and by paying careful attention to him, especially when he was driving, I had added some very colorful words to my vocabulary. Still, that excuse cut no ice with my mother, who proceeded to flog me to within an inch of my life. I'm a quick learner, and whenever she would question me about my language on subsequent occasions, I would affect my most innocent expression and say, "Oh, Mother dear, you know I don't say ugly words anymore. That was those other boys, and I think you should tell their mothers on them."

Any intimidation I might have felt from doctors, nurses, and other medical personnel was squelched by being around them so much during my upbringing. This "familiarity breeds contempt" mind-set did not always work to my benefit. Like the time in 1972 when I was rear-ended by a speeding drunk. I had stopped to make a left turn, but due to oncoming traffic, I could not proceed. I watched with some trepidation as a vehicle traveling maybe fifty miles per hour approached the back of my state car. Then—*wham*! He struck the left rear corner of my car, totaling both vehicles and inflicting a gash in my scalp.

Ever been cut on the head? It bleeds like hell. The worst part of the ordeal was that on that day, I was dressed in a custom-made light-gray suit. For those too young to remember, the Hong Kong tailors used to make trips to American cities. They would sequester themselves in a local motel, and you could go there to be measured for clothes made to your exact measurements. They measured everything you could imagine, along with some you might not. For example, they asked me which side I "dressed" on. I had no idea at the time, but what they want to know is on which side of your pants zipper your, um, equipment hangs. They make that side slightly larger (although for me that wasn't necessary). People used to tell me that suit fit like it was made for me. Well, it was. And now it was being stained by my blood, which I was certain would not come out (it did).

Neither the drunk nor I was seriously injured; however, we both needed medical attention, and since neither of our cars was drivable, the investigating police officer summoned an ambulance to transport us to the emergency room. This was a small ambulance, with a bench along each side in the rear. This drunk and I sat facing each other, and every couple of blocks he would reach out, touch me on the knee, and say, "Shun, I'm real shorry about this." The third time he reached for me, I pulled my suit jacket back, exposing my sidearm, and said, "If you touch me one more time, I'm going to splatter your brains all over this ambulance." The driver ducked down behind his seat; later he told me, "I just knew you were gonna shoot that asshole."

Well, anyway, we arrive at the emergency room. I had told the police dispatcher to have Dr. Fred Johnson meet me there. We all called him Dr. Fred to differentiate him from his brother, Tucker Johnson, also a doctor. I removed my suit jacket, and before I climbed onto the examining table, I was relieved of my sidearm by an attendant. Seeing my pistol, Dr. Fred launched into this soliloquy about guns and how parole officers should not be carrying them. All things considered, this had not been one of the better days of my life, and I finally snapped. I said, "Dr. Fred, how about if I enforce the law and you sew, okay?" I could almost see my words hanging in the air between us, like the speech bubble in a newspaper cartoon, and I would truly have loved to have them back. Why? Well, Dr. Fred was about to begin sewing up my head, and I had the sinking feeling that I had just guaranteed myself a *lot* of stitches, all of which would have to be (painfully) removed at some future date. I was right.

I have always been a fairly healthy person; however, 1983 was not a good year for me. In January of that year, I was hospitalized with five duodenal ulcers, all bleeding. May have had something to do with the fact that I was drinking half a quart of whiskey every night and smoking two to three packs of cigarettes daily, but I don't know. It was brought home to me how serious my condition was when a gastroenterologist whom I had never met stopped by my room to explain a proposed course of treatment. The first words out of his mouth, before he even introduced himself, were, "If you live." Even though quite sick, I was still full of piss and vinegar, so I looked at him and said, "Doctor, where were you the day they gave the class on bedside manner?" He left.

The next day, while I was eating my lunch, this little guy who looked like he had just started shaving came into my room, opened my pajama top, and again without even introducing himself, drew an imaginary line vertically down my torso with his finger, and said, "I'm going to start cutting here, then—" I stopped him with "Excuse me, but just who the hell are you?" He looked surprised, as though he was sure his reputation had preceded him, and replied, "Oh, I'm Dr. Chick Anderson." I said, "Well, Dr. Chick Anderson, not to hurt your feelings, but if anybody cuts me open, it'll be Dr. Fred Johnson." Anderson replied, "Dr. Johnson has the flu. I'm his assistant." I said, "Well, Dr. Chick Anderson, no offense, but I'd rather have Dr. Johnson sick than you well." He also left.

All this time, the hospital staff was pumping blood into me as fast as my body could accept it. I took eight pints in two days. I always tell people I had a complete oil change. On the second day of transfusions, this young nurse came into my room with a fresh bag of blood. I was reading a news magazine, and I told her, "You know, I've just been reading where scientists are experimenting with the use of animal plasma for humans in situations where a lot of blood is needed, like a battlefield [this was true]." I continued, "Do you suppose I'm getting any animal blood?" She looked genuinely shocked and replied, "No, of course not. Why do you ask?" I said, "Well, if it was animal blood, I wanted to make a special request." The nurse eyed me suspiciously; by now, she was beginning to realize she was being spoofed. She said, "Okay, I'll bite. What kind did you want?" I said, "Well, see, I can't swim, so I wondered if maybe some blood from a Labrador retriever…" I trailed off, and she said, "We need to get you well so we can get you OUT of here."

That little episode shot the hell out of January 1983. Then, in May, I developed a rapid, irregular heartbeat. My attending physician could not pinpoint the cause, so he had me admitted to the hospital—on the cardiac care unit! Interesting place: the patient in the room next to mine died one night. I knew this because I heard a code blue for his room go out over the intercom. This is hospital jargon meaning, "Hey, this joker just croaked. Bring the crash cart—NOW!" Sure enough, this special team came hauling butt down the hall and zapped the guy twice with a defibrillator, just like on television. Wow! Brought him back too.

Since they didn't really know what was wrong with me, they had me hooked up to a continuous electrocardiogram. I had wires stuck all over my chest, and the nurses could keep tabs on my condition right at their station. There was a small monitor just above my head so I could watch my own heartbeat. Talk about boring.

Then one day, while I was lying in bed minding my own business, I took a deep breath, and one of the wires popped loose from my chest. I looked up real quickly at the monitor, and it had flatlined. Now, I don't know if you have ever seen a dead body, but they don't have their eyes closed like they are just sleeping. No, that's just the way they are portrayed on the tube. Fact is, their eyes and mouth are wide open.

Knowing this, I opened my own eyes and mouth and fell back on my bed, waiting. I figured the crash cart team would come running in any second, at which point I would sit up and say, "Hey, what's the fuss?" Well, nothing happened. Ten minutes went by, and

I was sorely pissed. I pressed my call button, and this disembodied voice said, "Can I help you?" I replied, "I doubt it. I've been dead for ten minutes. But one thing you can do: get my doctor in here because I'm leaving."

The cardiologist, Dr. Finklestein, came by that evening to discharge me, explaining first that I had a minor heart condition. Minor heart condition? Now there's an oxymoron for you. I don't care if it's a pimple on my heart, if it's *my heart,* it ain't minor.

Sort of like the time I had had arthroscopic surgery on one of my knees. My neighbor, Danny Landers, saw me out cutting my grass and said, "Hey, didn't you just have knee surgery?" When I replied in the affirmative, he said, "Must have been minor." I said, "Danny, I'm going to tell you something important, so listen closely." Danny looked at me like I was about to reveal to him one of the great secrets of the universe. I said, "The only minor surgery is surgery performed on somebody else." I mean, when the anesthesiologist or nurse anesthetist who is going to put you to sleep has you sign a release saying that that you won't be upset if what they do kills you, things have passed right through minor, at least in my book.

The last story in this chapter is not really about a practical joke, but I couldn't find anywhere else to put it, and it's too funny to omit.

In the mid-1970s, the federal government was handing out fistfuls of money to law enforcement agencies, especially for advanced education. Since all of our officers already had at least a bachelor's degree, the parole board decided that it would be nice for some us to obtain our master's. They contracted with one of the state universities to set up a master's program just for us, and about thirty of us signed up for it. The only cost to us was for our books and supplies, and we were granted three days per month educational leave. Of course, we had to do *lots* of research and practicum work in addition to the classroom training. Still, it was a pretty sweet deal. The only catch was that for two years after receiving your degree, you had to continue to work in some law enforcement capacity—which I planned to do anyway—or pay back your tuition cost.

We had three primary instructors, all Ph.Ds, whom we called by their first names (hey, we were about as old as they were; besides, we were way past the age when a Ph.D degree impressed us). One of the three was a short bearded guy named Sonny Dortch. Sonny was a disciple of the touchy-feely school of counseling, and he decided that it might be nice for us to take a trust walk. For those of you who have never participated in one of these, here's how it works: First, you split up into pairs. Then one of you must close his eyes and pretend to be blind. He places his hand on his partner's arm (you have probably seen *real* blind people do this), and the "sighted" person takes the "blind" one for a walk. This wouldn't be so bad except for one restriction: neither of you can talk! Any communication between you must be nonverbal.

Well, I got paired with my boss, a middle-aged man named Jake Lampkin. Jake volunteered to be "blind" first. At the end of ten minutes, we were to switch places. Now, the main campus of this university we were enrolled in was located in the southern part of the state; however, the branch we were attending was right in the heart of a major city. So naturally, when fifteen "handicapped" couples hit the street en masse, we drew some curious stares. The funniest one I saw was a male meter maid. Back then, these were sworn police officers who rode scooters and handed out parking tickets. One of them was working the street where we were walking, and he had literally stopped and was staring, open-mouthed, at us. I knew what he was thinking: "Why the hell didn't somebody tell me the convention of the blind was in town?" As we passed by him, I couldn't resist a little humor, so I pointed to my "blind" charge and said, "I told him not to park there."

We had arrived at a corner and were stopped, waiting for the traffic light to change before crossing the street. Now remember, Jake had his eyes closed, and I was not allowed to tell him where we were. In an attempt to let him know we were at a curb and would be stepping down, I removed Jake's hand from my arm and pushed down on it vigorously a couple of times. Jake nodded, as though he understood. He didn't.

We began walking, but Jake did not step down. As a result, he fell flat on his ass. He was a good sport though. He never said a word but got up and started walking as if nothing had happened. However, when we came to the next corner, I repeated my nonverbal signal to step down. Jake obviously got the message this time; when the light changed, he stuck his right foot out in front of him and began pawing at the ground like a trick pony counting out his age. He was going to find that blessed curb this time.

When Jake's ten minutes of torment had passed, we swapped places. You've probably heard that the other four senses of blind people get keener to compensate for their disability. Believe it! In just a couple of minutes, my hearing had improved dramatically. I heard footsteps approaching on my right, followed by a voice saying, "Lawd, he a fine young man to be in a fix like that. How long he been like that?"

I couldn't suppress a smile as I waited for Jake to explain that I wasn't really blind, that this was just a school exercise. But oddly, he gave no response. In just a second, the unidentified voice said, "Oh! Oh…well…God bless you both then," and he was gone. After my ten minutes in the barrel, I said, "Jake, why the heck didn't you tell that dude what we were doing?" Jake had a gravelly, nasal voice, and he replied, "Well, Sonny said we weren't supposed to talk, so when he asked me that, I just shook my head and pointed to my mouth." I laughed so hard I almost wet myself, but I couldn't help thinking about the stranger who would have a great story to tell his grandchildren—about the day he saw the mute leading the blind!

Order in the Court

The largest part of a probation and parole officer's job is conducting background investigations on criminals for courts and the parole board. Most judges require that the officer who prepared the report of investigation on a particular individual be present for sentencing. This has a two-fold benefit: the officer hears the sentence imposed, along with any special conditions of probation, and can then prepare an order of probation for the judge's signature, and the officer is able to answer questions that may arise at the sentencing hearing from either the judge or the defense attorney. This is a very convenient arrangement for the court; however, these hearings and the associated investigations do consume most of an officer's time. In the locations where I worked, officers were assigned to a particular judge, and it was normal to get to know that judge and his or her expectations well.

Judge Greg Ross was several years younger than I. He was born with a silver spoon in his mouth and had had little courtroom experience, especially representing criminals, before being appointed judge. Because of his limited contact with the lower strata of society, his comprehension of street language was somewhat lacking. Judge Ross was aware of my experience and often relied on me to interpret for him what a defendant was saying. During the colloquy before sentencing an individual on a guilty plea, a judge must clearly ascertain that a defendant knows what he is doing and that he is actually guilty of the offense to which he is pleading. Judge Ross would say to the defendant, "Tell me what you did that makes you guilty of this charge."

One day, the judge had a young man wanting to plead guilty to an assault charge. He asked the fellow to explain what he had done, and the defendant replied, "Me an' my homeboy was study [steady] talkin', right? Den dis udder dude come up an' he say, 'Hey, mu-fu, whut be de rap?'" The defendant continued in this vein for several minutes, and it was clear from the judge's expression that he had no idea what this guy was talking about. As soon as the young man finished with his version of the offense, the judge looked at me. I knew that he wanted me to explain what the defendant meant, so I said, "He said, 'Me an' my homeboy was study talkin', right?'" If looks could kill, I would not be writing this right now. Finally, I couldn't keep a straight face any longer, so I gave the judge a synopsis of the dude's statement—in English!

Judge Ross's father, Wendell, was a local attorney of some prominence. He was quite proud of the fact that he was close friends with the governor and other high-ranking officials. In those days, there was a small snack bar on the first floor of the courthouse, and it was a very democratic place. It was not uncommon to see judges, attorneys, and yes, even the lowly probation and parole officer eating or drinking coffee at the same table. Joe Cornell was another local attorney, and he was a practical joker par excellence. One day he and Mr. Ross were sitting at the same table, and Mr. Ross was talking about the impending nuptials of the governor's youngest daughter. It seems that while several hundred dignitaries had been invited to the reception, the size of the church had dictated that only about a hundred could attend the wedding, and Mr. Ross announced to those assembled that he was one of that select group.

Now, Joe waited until the conversation had progressed to another topic, then he said, "Ross, I've got to have some new business cards made. Can I see one of yours?" Mr. Ross puffed up and handed Joe one of his cards. Joe said, "Wow! Those are really nice. Would you mind if I patterned mine after yours?" Well, now Mr. Ross was about to burst with pride, so he gave Joe the okay. And what did Joe do with Mr. Ross's card? Why, he proceeded to a downtown dime store, where he purchased a large pack of paper plates. He then took these to a high-end downtown jewelry store where he had done a lot of business, handed them the paper plates and Ross's business card, and had them wrapped and delivered to the governor's mansion!

J. Robert Thames was appointed a judge at a young age. He and I had graduated from high school in the same class, and until he became His Honor, he was just Robby to me. Robby was a bright guy, and he was intent on starting some progressive new programs in the local criminal justice system. One day he had a pregnant defendant standing in front of his bench, and in an attempt to decide whether to incarcerate her or whether that might impose an undue hardship and financial burden on the jail, he asked her, "Just how pregnant are you?" Of course, he expected her answer to be a certain number of months. Instead, she smiled sweetly at him and replied, "Totally." I made a hasty exit from the courtroom. I'm sure Judge Thames wished he could do the same.

When he reached middle age, Judge Thames became quite religious, and he would witness to anybody who would listen. One day I was having lunch alone at a downtown restaurant when Judge Thames asked if he could dine with me. Naturally I said yes. He began to witness, which was okay by me. I am a devout Christian and can witness with the best of them. So there we were, eating and witnessing, witnessing and eating. Oh Lord, we were on our game. If we had issued an invitation right then, I think we could have led half the patrons in the restaurant to salvation. Then, Robby came to the punch line (knowing him, I knew there would be one). He said, "I don't know why I came over here today. The Lord just told me to." I replied, "Really? Did He also tell you I'm not going to buy your lunch?"

As with Robby, I had known Sid Turner long before he was appointed to the bench. Sid had a real paranoid streak, and when he got agitated, he would stutter. One day he and I were talking over coffee in the courthouse cafeteria when Sid said, "S-S-Somebody b-broke in m-m-my office last night." He then proceeded to detail what the offender had taken and that he, or they, had ransacked the place. Then Sid got this dark look on his face and lowered his voice almost to a whisper. After looking around the room to be sure nobody was eavesdropping, he continued, in the same conspiratorial tone, "I th-th-think they knew me." I asked, "Why, Sid?" He replied, "B-b-before they left, they sh-sh-shit on the floor."

I'm pretty good at maintaining my composure, but I lost it that time. It was rumored that Sid kept a pistol handy while he was holding court. I never attempted to verify that information; however, I was always a little nervous when standing in front of his bench.

I appeared in many courtrooms during my career, fortunately not as a defendant (well, once, but that's another story). Some courtrooms were elaborate, with polished paneling on the walls, touches of marble, and a tall, imposing bench for the judge. Others were quite simple.

I was stationed with the parole board in the western part of the state for several months, and I served the court of a judge who had three rural counties in his circuit. It was necessary for him to hold court in each of the three counties on a regular basis. One of these counties was listed as the second poorest in the United States, and its county seat reflected that poverty. The courthouse square was comprised of several stone buildings, all constructed shortly after the end of the Civil War. You could stand in front of the courthouse and hear the prisoners in the jail a block away singing black spirituals, the kind where the leader sings a line and the others repeat it. Had it not been for vehicular traffic around the square, you could easily have imagined that you were a hundred years back in time.

The courtroom was on the second floor of the ancient courthouse and was accessed by either a rickety stairwell or a metal fire escape that was barely hanging on to the outer wall of the building. There was no air conditioning; however, the courtroom did have high ceilings with several fans suspended from them. In addition, on two of the walls were several sets of French doors that could be opened to provide ventilation. Problem was, there were no screens on the doors, so along with the breeze came an assortment of bugs, many of them wasps. The judge's bench consisted of a small dais, maybe a foot high; on top of which was an old teacher's desk. Our court system required its judges to wear robes when conducting court, so you can imagine how hot it got for the judge in this courtroom.

Judge Clyde Norton was a really nice guy who conducted his court very informally. Between conversations among the spectators and the noise of traffic (particularly log trucks) circling the square below, it was necessary to be in close proximity to the bench if you wanted to know what was going on. One day Judge Norton was right in the middle of sentencing a criminal defendant when he sort of flinched and stopped talking. His face got a little pale, and he adjourned court temporarily. Concerned that he might be ill, I followed him out the room's rear door.

There was no judge's chamber in this courtroom, just a landing beside a bathroom that had apparently not been cleaned since Methuselah was a teenager. Judge Norton was doubled over in obvious pain, and I was alarmed. I said, "Judge, what's wrong?" He moaned a couple of times, then replied, "One of those damn wasps got me." These wasps were about the size of a hummingbird, and I had had an encounter with one myself, so I knew it was no laughing matter. I asked, "Where did he sting you?" Judge Norton looked at me with a grimace. I don't think he really wanted to say, but he finally replied, "In the DAMN CROTCH, that's where!" I know it wasn't funny, but I just lost it.

People who haven't spent time in front of a variety of judges probably think that they are all stiff-upper-lip stuffed shirts. And some of them are. But others are downright human, especially when not on the bench. J. B. Walker loved to tell about the time that he, as a parole board district supervisor, went to visit Tim Smith, an officer of long standing who worked in a small town in the eastern part of the state. The way JB told it, he and Tim were walking down the central hall of that county's courthouse when Tim hailed this distinguished-looking man on the other side of the hallway with "Hey, you old son of a bitch!" To which, according to JB, this gentleman replied, "Hello there, you old bastard. How's it going?" As they continued walking, JB asked Tim, "Who was that?" Much to JB's shock, Tim replied, "Oh, that's just the circuit judge."

One of the counties that J.B. supervised contained a large city with a correspondingly big probation and parole office. Henry Barton was one of the officers assigned to that location. Now, Henry was a drunk. He was what you call a spree drinker. He would stay sober for months—or even years—at a time, then he would go on a bender and drink until he had to be hospitalized. Henry had worked for the parole board for many years and was well-liked, but not by his fellow officers, most of whom were recent hires. They complained that Henry's hospitalizations, which were allegedly for heart problems, were causing a burden because they had to handle his workload while he was incapacitated. They decided to complain to J.B. and ask him to file charges on Henry and seek his ouster.

Well, J.B. knew Henry well, but he decided to investigate the situation before acting. He went to the local presiding judge and asked his opinion. The judge was incensed that these newer officers did not have the proper respect for Henry and his long record of service to his court and the parole board. So he told JB, "You go back and tell those sons of bitches that I'd rather have Henry Barton drunk than all the rest of their worthless asses sober." 'Nuff said.

I had a good friend who was a state trooper. One night, he arrested a guy and charged him with making an obscene gesture. It seems the man had flipped him off. When the case was heard in district court, the judge decided that "shooting a bird" at someone was not actually an obscene gesture, so he dismissed the charge. My friend was incredulous, and as he turned to leave the courtroom, he stopped and said, "Judge, are you absolutely sure that's not an obscene gesture?"

The judge was somewhat irritated at being questioned, and he replied, "Yes, trooper, I'm positive." I wasn't in court that day, but I learned from fellow officers what happened next. According to the accounts I heard, my trooper friend raised his arm, formed a perfect "bird," and said, "I'll see you later, Judge." I'm sure the judge would have liked to have held him in contempt of court, but seeing how he had just ruled that giving somebody the finger was not a crime, his hands were tied. Word got back to trooper headquarters though, and they decided that because of this incident, the trooper might experience difficulty working with this judge (ya think?), so they transferred him to a duty station in another part of the state.

Defense attorneys always loved putting the probation officer who had conducted the presentence investigation on their client on the witness stand, hoping to discredit all or some of the report and thus portray their client in a more favorable light for sentencing purposes. This happened to me with my very first sentencing hearing. The attorney was very aggressive and insinuated a number of times that I had not produced an accurate report.

We were in the courtroom of Judge Elrod Hardy, who was thought by most of us to be a little nuts (several years later, His Honor was sentenced to a term of twenty years in the state penitentiary for accepting bribes). The person to be sentenced was a young man by the name of Cleophus Barnes. He was seated, unshackled, at a table directly in front of Judge Hardy, and standing beside him was a sheriff's deputy who was routinely assigned the task of escorting prisoners from the jail to a courtroom. Carter (we never used his first name) was a huge man, about six six, and was all muscle, so he never had any trouble with the inmates.

Without warning, the courtroom lights went out. Now, this was an interior room without windows, so when the lights were off, it was pitch-black. Judge Hardy asked, in a voice tinged with obvious concern, "Mr. Carter, do you have the prisoner?" Carter replied calmly in the affirmative, and at about the same time, the lights came back on, revealing Carter standing beside Cleophus with his hand on the defendant's shoulder.

The defense attorney resumed his assault on my report. This did not bother me, as I had been a juvenile probation officer before accepting my current position and was familiar with the courtroom antics of lawyers. Well, about this time, the lights went out again. This time, Judge Hardy was unable to conceal the panic in his voice, as he almost shouted, "Carter…Carter?" Cue the lights, and there stood Carter, again with his hand resting on Barnes's shoulder.

I told a colleague later that I would have given a serious amount of money for a remote control so that I could have extinguished the lights, whereupon I would have shouted, "Get him, Cleophus!" I truly believe Judge Hardy would have done a swan dive over the front of that bench trying to get away.

Unlike some of my contemporaries, I always enjoyed sparring—verbally, of course—with attorneys. One such match happened between me and Robert Feinbaum, who happened to be a friend of mine. He and I had collaborated on the legal framework for the formation of a union of state employees and had visited in each other's homes. Nevertheless, on this particular day, he was not happy with me. He was representing a man who had pled guilty to first-degree theft, a crime punishable by up to twenty years' confinement.

This offender was operating an interstate stolen car ring, and his house was completely furnished with stolen property. But the worst part of it was that he was the captain of the guards, a high-ranking position, at one of our state prisons. Now, I have no respect for a crook who hides behind a badge. Be a cop or be a criminal, but don't mix the two. That does nothing but tarnish the reputation of the profession I was sworn to uphold.

So anyway, we were in court for the sentencing, and I was recommending the maximum, twenty years. Robert was attacking my presentence report in front of a courtroom packed with spectators when Judge John Phillips stopped the interrogation. Covering his microphone with his hand, he leaned over to me in the witness chair and asked me if I felt like Feinbaum was badgering me. Judge Phillips and I went way back also. When I was a training officer at our departmental academy, I had invited him to speak to several different classes of officers concerning changes in our state's court system. I have a bass voice, and it normally carries well unamplified. Still, for the benefit of the spectators, I raised my volume a few decibels and replied, "A lightweight like him?"

As soon as he was able to compose himself and call the laughing courtroom back to order, Judge Phillips gestured for Robert to continue. Feinbaum's face had turned as red as the butt of a boiled lobster. I was actually afraid he might have a stroke, but he managed to sputter, "Objection!" Judge Phillips looked at him and said, "To what, Mr. Feinbaum? That conversation was not on record." Robert's client got the twenty years he deserved, and Robert and I are still friends. Sort of.

Not all judges held probation officers in such high esteem. An example was Judge Peter Harper. Like many judges, he was involved in various community activities and was respected by those who really didn't know him. Many folks outside the court system did not know, for instance, that Judge Harper had decided to mentor a career criminal named Mark Stevens. Harper felt that with his overestimated intellect and his powerful (in his mind) influence, he could change Stevens into an upstanding citizen.

Accordingly, although he had to sentence Stevens to a penitentiary term, Judge Harper asked the county sheriff to allow Stevens to serve his time in the county jail. Now, this was not completely without precedent. If, say, the sheriff had a state inmate who was a good cook, sometimes arrangements were made for him—or her—to serve time locally. In the case of Mark Stevens, however, Judge Harper just wanted to keep him close at hand in order to try to remake him into Joe Citizen. Stevens repaid the kindness Judge Harper had foolishly extended him by kidnapping and murdering a young female court reporter. You need to know what an arrogant and misinformed judge of character Harper was in order to appreciate the next story.

Clearly without a clue as to the part his poor assessment of criminal character had played in the Stevens debacle, Harper allowed himself to get way too close to another career criminal, Jack Bishop. Bishop was a low-life thug who clearly overestimated his limited intelligence. I had supervised Bishop on a previous conviction from another state, so I knew him well. His only desire in life was to become an accomplished con artist while portraying himself to gullible people like Judge Harper as a victim of his guideless upbringing. He was even a member of a semiorganized crime syndicate referred to by local law enforcement officers as the Dixie Mafia.

Well, Bishop was charged with a new felony, and just by the luck of the draw, I was assigned to conduct a presentence investigation on him for Judge Harper. To say that the resulting report was unfavorable would be akin to saying that the Titanic encountered a little trouble on its maiden voyage. I called Bishop everything but a child of God. Harsh? Yes, but I could back up every word.

Lo and behold, I strolled into work the Monday after presenting my report. As usual, I was hung over and not in the mood for a truckload of crap, but that's what was coming my way. My boss Dave Drollet walked in with my report, threw it on my desk, and said, "Judge Harper says this is the most biased report he has ever read, and I agree with him. Rewrite it."

There were many times in my life when I had to take a deep breath before beginning a response with "Go to hell." This was one of those occasions. Finally I said, "Really? Well, you can tell Judge Harper for me that the report is not biased. It's one-sided, and when a person has only one side, that's all I can present. And by the way, Dave, if you want the report rewritten, do it yourself. My report stands as written."

Please don't think that I mentally categorize all people convicted of criminal offenses as beyond rehabilitation. Many of them, with or without a parole and probation officer's guidance, recognize the error of their ways and become good citizens you would be happy to have as neighbors. However, some are just sorry and worthless, and you have to be able to recognize those and call a spade a spade. One such dirtbag was Darrel Black. Darrel was the son of a former police officer who had been terminated (I never knew the reason). He had four brothers, and at one time or another, I had had all but one of them on probation or parole. The only reason I had never had the youngest was that he was only twelve years old.

Darrel was a drug addict, and most of his criminal convictions were drug-related. The last time I had any personal contact with him, I was assigned to conduct a presentence investigation on him due to a drug charge to which he had entered a plea of guilty. On the date of his sentencing, Darrell appeared in front of Judge Deke Crosby, who had been the county district attorney for many years before being appointed to the bench. Judge Crosby decided to read aloud to Darrel my sentencing recommendation. Word for word, it said: "Darrell Black belongs to the very scum of society and should not be allowed to freely walk the streets of this city, where he can further contaminate the morals of any decent human being who has the misfortune to come into contact with him." Hey, if you're gonna shoot them down, shoot them down in flames.

Well, Darrel got sent to the penitentiary—but that's not the end of the story. After a few years, he finished his time and was released. One night he called me at my home. Clearly under the influence of alcohol and/or some other intoxicating substance, he slurred, "I don't like what you said about me in that report, and you're gonna pay for it." I responded, "Ooh, Darrel, I'll lie awake all night worrying about that." I figured he was just blowing smoke. Still, just in case something did happen to me, I made his threat known to my superiors and to the local police department.

A very few days later, Darrel Black was killed. Seems he ran off a city street at a high rate of speed and slammed into a brick wall. His body was found in the back seat of the car. Now, that in itself was not really suspicious. Violent vehicle crashes often result in the ejection of the driver from his seat. What was a little strange, though, was that investigating officers found a brick on the front floorboard of Darrel's car. Had someone used it to weigh down the accelerator? They didn't know. But it seemed that everybody with whom I had contact in the next week or so had heard about the mysterious circumstances surrounding his death, and it was routine for them to say, "Didn't you and Darrel have words just before his death? Hmmm…"

When I first met Bobby MacAnnely, I was struck by what an unlikely criminal he was. The young man had two college degrees and a well-paying professional job. What brought him into contact with me was that he had entered a plea of guilty to one count of second-degree assault, and I had been instructed to perform a presentence investigation for the court.

It seems that MacAnnely had gone to the home of his estranged wife. After they ate dinner, he asked her to reconcile with him, and when she refused, he picked up a baseball bat and proceeded to beat her severely. As she lay in a pool of her own blood, she pleaded with him to summon medical assistance, and he agreed, on the condition that she would not prosecute him. Among her many injuries, one of her elbows was so badly shattered that it had to be replaced with an artificial joint. Boy was a real prince.

Well, this was another of those crimes that was so heinous, I felt the maximum sentence of twenty years was called for, and I so stated in my report. MacAnnely was represented by Geoff Baker, an attorney of regional prominence who had previously represented two governors. He was not somebody to be taken lightly. At the sentencing hearing, he presented, as an excuse for his client's violence, the allegation that MacAnnely suffered from hypoglycemia. The term actually means low blood sugar, as opposed to hyperglycemia (high blood sugar), commonly called diabetes. A person with hypoglycemia is subject to precipitous drops in blood sugar, which results in weakness, shakiness, and occasionally, fainting. Baker represented to the court that on the night of the assault, MacAnnely and the victim had consumed a take-out dinner of fried chicken and mashed potatoes. He claimed that the potatoes turned rapidly to sugar and that, when that left his bloodstream, MacAnnely became uncontrollably angry.

I listened patiently to this attempt to portray MacAnnely as a victim of his sugar-starved impulses. As soon as Mr. Baker concluded his remarks and his plea for leniency for MacAnnely, I requested permission to address the court. I said, "Judge, I also have hypoglycemia. Had it for years. And I can assure the court that if Mr. MacAnnely did suffer a drop in his blood sugar, he would not have had the strength to inflict the injuries he did. In any event, chicken is loaded with protein and would have offset the potatoes." Judge Ross looked at the attorney and queried, "Anything else, Mr. Baker?" Baker lowered his head, gave an exasperated sigh, and replied, "I guess not." Twenty years. Case closed.

Judge Rick Everett was in his late forties. He was a handsome man, tall and slim, with a shock of blond hair. He was in high demand as a public speaker and was the darling of the community, especially the ladies. I think it would be safe to say that he was regarded as a pillar of society and a champion of moral values. That is, until he left his wife and family and moved to another state with a girl young enough to be his daughter. But that's another story.

Andy Grant was about thirty years old. He was the first black officer ever hired by the parole board (remember, this was in the early 1970s), but he was already known in the state. Several years earlier, Andy's father, acting on Andy's behalf, had sued the school board in a neighboring county for racial discrimination, ultimately leading to the desegregation of that county's schools. When he came to us, Andy had a major league chip on his shoulder. Apparently he was aware that his reputation as a civil rights litigant had preceded him, and he expected us to treat him like a pariah, which we never did. Andy was quite intelligent; however, like the rest of us, he was capable of making mistakes.

One day, one of our secretaries was typing one of Andy's reports destined for Judge Everett's court. Suddenly, she jerked the earphones from her ears, threw them down on her desk, and began laughing hysterically. We all gathered around her desk, but she was still laughing too hard to tell us what had happened. Frank Sharp, the officer-in-charge, picked up the earphones to listen to the tape, and he started laughing so hard that big tears were rolling down his cheeks. One by one, we had the opportunity to listen to the part of the tape that had set the secretary off.

In summarizing the details of the offense to which this defendant had pled guilty, Andy had said, "Mr. Jones shot Ms. Smith once, just above the left titty." The secretary asked Sharp if she should change Andy's wording. Sharp, not being overly fond of Andy, said, "No, let it go to the judge just like that."

Now, Judge Everett was quite intelligent, and like many bright people, he was a multitasker. I learned this while observing him during a high-profile murder case. Photographers had been banned from the court proceedings; however, the newspaper's political cartoonist, an accomplished artist, was allowed in. On day two of the trial, a sketch appeared on the front page of the paper bearing the caption: "Judge Everett strikes a thoughtful pose during Stigart trial." The drawing showed Judge Everett looking down, one hand against his head.

Well, I was standing beside the judge's bench and could see what he was doing during this "thoughtful" time. He was reading a paperback book, which he was holding near his lap, out of view of the spectators. The reason he was holding his hand to his head was that one of the earpieces was missing from his glasses, and he was too cheap to buy another pair! Occasionally, the defendant's lawyer, unhappy with the prosecution's line of questioning, would jump out of his chair and shout, "Objection!" Judge Everett would look up, ponder his response for a moment, then reply either "Sustained" or "Overruled." I am convinced to this day that he had no idea as to the substance of the objection.

Many judges like to receive the probation and parole officer's presentence reports a day or two prior to sentencing. This gives them time to study the information about the criminal defendant and formulate an appropriate sentence. Not Judge Everett. He wanted us to hand the presentence report to him while the defendant was standing before him. He would then speed read the report (actually, we were all aware that he concentrated on the defendant's prior record and the details of the charge to which he was pleading; the person's personal history background held little interest for him) and impose sentence. During that time, all sentencing was done on one day; therefore, all of us were in court at the same time. We had a court docket showing which defendants were to be sentenced and in what order.

Andy's defendant was called, and he approached the bench. Andy handed his report to the judge, who began reading. The rest of us officers were seated in the jury box, to the right of the judge. Judge Everett struck his usual "thoughtful" pose, his left hand holding his one-legged glasses up to his eyes. All of a sudden, he dropped his glasses on the bench and turned slowly to face us. He was making a manful attempt to control his emotions, but the corners of his mouth were twitching like someone having a seizure, and a tiny tear trickled down one cheek. This was more than I could stand, so I jumped up and exited the courtroom—hastily!

In Andy's defense, let me say that he was not the only one of us who occasionally made a faux pas in a report. Our presentence reports were in narrative form, and most of us had pat phrases that we used in the more mundane sections like, say, health or employment history. As I mentioned earlier, our offices at this time were essentially cubicles, making it virtually impossible not to overhear what the officer in the next office was saying.

One day, I was dictating a report when I heard the officer whose cubicle was next to mine begin laughing so hard that he was gasping for breath. At the time, I had no idea about the source of his mirth. That is, until he walked into my office and said, "You need to play back the details of the offense that you just dictated." Now this defendant had entered a plea of guilty to an assault. He had shot his girlfriend while they were both inside a local nightspot called the

Fun Box. So it seemed quite natural to dictate the following: "Mr. Jones shot Ms Smith in the Fun Box." That's the kind of thing that happens when you're dictating while your mind is a thousand miles away.

We had a young female parole officer named Earline Gentry. Earline was a natural blonde, and while she was really pretty intelligent, she was prone to make the kinds of statements from which blonde jokes are derived. When she came to work for the parole board, Earline was living with her boyfriend, whom she later married. In addition to the front door through which the public entered, our office suite had a back door that we employees used since our parking lot was behind the building. Anyone entering or exiting via this portal would pass directly in front of my office, the door to which was usually open. One day, Earline came in and, seeing me seated at my desk, said, "Oh." Then she paused, apparently gathering her thoughts before continuing. "Well. I'm going to have a baby."

I was flattered that she had selected me to be the first in our office to know, even though I realized that it was only because I was the first person she had encountered. Knowing that she was not married at the time, I suspected that this pregnancy was an "oops." Still, she seemed content with her condition, so I offered my congratulations. Then I decided to inquire as to whether she knew the gender of the fetus.

Ever had really good intentions, but what you said just came out totally wrong? I said, "Do you know anything about sex?" Realizing that, being pregnant, she did have some knowledge of the subject, I hurriedly added, "Well, I guess you do." Fortunately—or unfortunately, depending on your point of view—the whole faux pas went right over Earline's head.

During my years as a city police officer, any arrest we made, other than a felony charge, was heard in the municipal court. Judge Mel Ziwicky was a very sharp young guy. He was quite personable when he was out of the courtroom, but on the bench he was all business. One morning, I was presenting arrest information on a defendant I had charged the previous night with DUI (driving under the influence). This guy was none too happy about being arrested, and on the way to the jail, he cussed me until a fly wouldn't have landed on me.

Now if you told Judge Ziwicky that a defendant had used abusive language, he required that you repeat exactly what the person had said. In the course of providing details of this arrest, I said, "Your Honor, on the way to the jail, the defendant directed a great deal of profane language toward the arresting officer [me]." Judge Ziwicky had his head down writing a jail commitment order on the person he had just sentenced. Without looking up, he said, "Officer Melton, you know you have to repeat what he said." I replied, "All of it?" I had been in Judge Ziwicky's courtroom many times before, and he knew that I was aware of the procedure. He raised his head, shot me a quizzical look, and said, "Yes! All of it." I shrugged my shoulders and said, "Okay. Well, he called me a goddamn, motherfucking, whore-hopping son of a bitch."

The courtroom was packed that day, and if someone had produced a sound meter at just that moment. I think the volume of laughter would have broken it. Judge Ziwizky turned a shade of red that can best be described as—purple. A few days later, I saw him in the county courthouse. He grabbed my arm and said (with a smile), "You set me up, you son of a bitch!" I couldn't do anything but laugh.

Judge Ziwicky had a full-time law practice. As with the other judges in municipal court, this was a part-time gig for him. One of the other judges was a female, Lakendra Wilson. She was aloof to the point of arrogance, which would have been a little more tolerable had she had a brain. Also, her disdain for police officers—especially those of a different race from hers—was on display whenever she was on the bench. Bring any kind of case in front of her, and you were subject to having your evidence dissected and critiqued, sometimes to the point of ridicule. She never wasted an opportunity to suggest that had she been present at the time of the arrest, things would have been handled differently. Did we hate the witch? Well, umm, yes.

Imagine my delight then, when, upon reporting for duty one morning, I learned that she had been arrested the night before—by one of our own officers (oh, the disgrace)—and charged with DUI. Seems that her vehicle had a mind of its own and had taken it upon itself to jump the curb and strike a utility pole. Not sure if she was disbarred, but she definitely lost her judgeship. I ran into her about a month later. My greeting in such a situation in the past would have been, "Good morning, Your Honor." What I did say was not my fault; the devil made me do it. I smiled and said, "Hey, Lakendra, what kind of car did you get to replace that Lincoln you trashed? Oh, that's right, you can't drive yet, can you [upon being convicted of DUI, she had lost her license]? Sorry, I forgot [right]." Hey, what goes around comes around.

Every city I ever worked in as a probation and parole officer had its share of courthouse characters. In the early 1970s, I was assigned to a major southern city. The district attorney for the circuit was a sixtyish gentleman named Deke Crosby, and the circuit court clerk was Jack Martin, a man in his late seventies. Deke and Jack were long-time friends, and the banter between them was often hilarious.

One day, I was in court while criminal defendants were being arraigned (entering a plea). The defendant's rights in a court proceeding were not as clearly defined back then as they are today. While it takes a modern-day judge several minutes to go through a colloquy with a defendant, making sure he understands what he is charged with and that he is entering his plea voluntarily, the system in those days was to line the defendants up like cattle going through a chute. As each came before the bench, he was asked only two questions: Do you have a lawyer, and how do you plead?

This was the era when many black people wore their hair in an afro, a large bushy style. Deke was standing before the bench arraigning the individuals, while Mr. Jack, as everyone called him, was seated just behind them at a table. Mr. Jack was almost totally deaf, and when he thought he was whispering, he was actually speaking loudly enough to be heard several feet away. As a black female wearing the largest afro I had ever seen approached the bench, Mr. Jack "whispered" to Deke, "Damn, Deke, look at the hair on that heifer!" Proceedings were interrupted momentarily while we all composed ourselves.

Mr. Jack had known Judge Everett since the judge was a baby, and he occasionally forgot his courtroom manners. One day, Judge

Everett announced to the defendants and attorneys assembled for arraignment that he was making a change to the standard arraignment procedure. Apparently, Mr. Jack perceived that this change would have a negative impact on his office. He charged the bench, shouting, "Now, Judge, you can't do that! You know we agreed..." Judge Everett attempted—politely, at first—to cut Mr. Jack off and explain why he wanted to make this change but to no avail; Mr. Jack couldn't hear him. He continued to rant, loudly and somewhat disrespectfully. Finally Judge Everett raised his voice to a level that could have been heard in the next county and said, "Mr. Martin, the court will not TOLERATE any further disrespect from the circuit court clerk!"

Well, Mr. Jack heard that, and he realized that the judge could rightfully cite him for contempt. Still, it was clear that his feelings were hurt. He had helped raise this whippersnapper, and he felt entitled to preferential treatment. He said "All right"—actually very quietly—and returned to his seat. In a minute, though, once again under the false impression that he was whispering, he said, "Son of a bitch!" Thankfully, Judge Everett ignored that one.

Elwood Schmidt was one of the most colorful lawyers I have ever known. He was tall, and he shaved his head, many years before that look became fashionable. His attire was always the same: three-piece suit, cowboy boots, and a white Stetson hat. One day, I was sitting in the conference room of the district attorney's office copying information I needed for a presentence report from one of their files. Elwood was there, along with Bob Hardy, the only assistant district attorney at that time. Bob was a young fellow. He was a transplant from New York and was the perfect foil for the blustery Southern Elwood, who was holding forth on his perceived courtroom expertise. He said, "Well, I'll tell ya one thing: Elwood has NEVAH lost a case!"

Now this was too much for Hardy. He jumped out of his chair and said, "Elwood, you know that's a lie! Why, I have personally won several cases that you defended. How can you tell a lie like that?" As he was about to find out, Hardy had been suckered. Elwood looked genuinely hurt (like most good attorneys, he had a rubber face that he could change at will) and said, "Why, Mr. Hardy, it seems apparent that you misunderstood the message I was attempting to convey." Standing with his thumbs hooked in the lapels of his suit coat, a typical Elwood pose, he continued, "You see, before I ever take a case to court, the long green crosses my palm. At that point, ELWOOD has WON the case. The defendant may go to prison for life, but ELWOOD has WON!"

Elwood was an old sot, but a likeable one. Since he was aware that most of us would take a drink on a special occasion—like, say, any day ending in *y*—he would bring each of us a bottle of whiskey at Christmas. Not rotgut, either—expensive stuff, better than I could afford to drink on a regular basis. We never considered this a bribe, and Elwood never asked for any special treatment in return. Some attorneys, however, were not above providing inducements in an attempt to influence an officer's decision.

Robert Brown had a bad reputation among the legal profession. He was a homosexual and would periodically attempt to find much younger males with whom to engage in sexual encounters. Usually, he wound up being beaten up and robbed. Of course, when he would report these assaults to the authorities, they always knew what had actually transpired. His conduct was so flagrant and disgraceful that he had been asked by the local bar association not to handle court cases, but he still did. His primary income was from his position as chief legal counsel to an agency of the state government.

I learned about Mr. Brown's sexual peccadilloes one day when he brought a criminal defendant he was representing to my office to be interviewed for a presentence investigation. We were assigned these investigations on a rotating basis, and my number was up. After introducing me to his client, Mr. Brown handed me a thick manila envelope, which he said contained letters of recommendation for the young man. It was not uncommon for attorneys to collect letters of this type, hoping that they might have a positive influence on the probation officer's sentencing recommendation and the judge's sentence. I did note that the envelope seemed awfully heavy to be filled with only paper. After he left the office, I opened the envelope and discovered that it contained a flat quart bottle of Beam's Best bourbon.

I was beside myself with anger. I carried the envelope and its contents to the presiding judge, who then filled me in on Mr. Brown's sordid past. The saddest part of his perversion was that he had a daughter who was also a lawyer and an elected official. Undoubtedly, his escapades caused her shame and embarrassment.

The judge suggested I call Mr. Brown and tell him to come get his bribe, which I did. After I had calmed down somewhat, the officer-in-charge, Frank Sharp, and I were having a few laughs about this demented attorney and his clumsy attempt at influence peddling. I said, "Yeah, the worst part is, it wasn't even my brand. Now, a case of good scotch might have made me think about it."

Hagreb Jihadi was born and raised in a Middle Eastern country. His father was closely allied with the dictator of that country, and when the dictator was deposed, all those associated with his government, including Hagreb's father, were killed. In order to avoid the same fate, Hagreb and his remaining family fled to the United States. Hagreb's family was well-to-do, and he was thus able to attend law school.

Hagreb spoke with a heavy accent, and his courtroom antics were the stuff of which legend is made. During the trial of a subject accused of murder, Hagreb, in order to demonstrate the low-light conditions at the time of the crime, switched off the courtroom lights. There were no windows in this room, and when the lights went off, the room was plunged into total darkness. The problem was that Hagreb had not notified Judge Ross of his intent to perform these theatrics, so no extra security precautions were in place. A murder defendant was seated—wearing no handcuffs or other restraints—at a table on which rested the alleged murder weapon! Judge Ross was not amused and held Hagreb in contempt.

And Hagreb had no concept of political correctness. Attempting to cast doubt on a witness's identification of his client, a young black man, Hagreb told Judge Ross, in open court, "They all look alike, you know."

Hagreb referred to all his clients—in court, at least—as "a goot boy." On one occasion, he was defending a young man accused of violating his probation. The alleged violation was that the defendant had been accused of a new charge of robbery. Hagreb told Judge Ross, "Chudge, dis is a goot boy. Dis vas not a rubbery. Vat happened vas dat he bought some drugs, and dey vere not vat he expected, so he demanded his money back." Judge Ross rarely expressed much emotion while on the bench, but that one clearly got him. He smiled and said, "Oh, I see. He didn't ROB anybody, he just bought drugs… while on PROBATION! Mr. Jihadi, does he have anything else to say before I revoke his probation?"

Hagreb had an arranged marriage to a lovely Middle Eastern woman who had been raised in the United States and spoke unaccented English. The marriage, however, was short-lived. At their divorce hearing, Hagreb did not feel that Judge Patty Gordon was being fair to him, so he snapped at her, "In my country, ve buy und sell vimmin like you effery day!" Not the wisest thing he could have said; however, Judge Gordon ignored him.

After the court hearing was over, Hagreb went to the back hallway of the courthouse, where he lay down on the floor in front of an exit door. He was clearly distraught, and no one was able to reason with him. Judge Robby Thames walked over, knelt beside him, and said in a tender, consoling voice, "Hagreb, you need some help. Get up and let me take you to the hospital." Hagreb's reply was "Chudge, you haf been very goot to me, but Chudge Gordon has done me wrong, and I am goink to lie here until I die or pass out!"

A truly good attorney is like an experienced real estate agent: he's not afraid to tell his client what changes need to be made in order to maximize the chances for a successful outcome. We used to marvel at the difference between a defendant's appearance at his arraignment and his look at sentencing. I can't count the times I've seen a skank transformed into a respectable-looking citizen, clearly due to the influence of the lawyer representing him. Nasty shaggy hair cut short and scraggly beard shaved, the man who, at his arraignment, you could pretty clearly identify as a criminal defendant would appear for sentencing wearing a white shirt and conservative tie. I have even seen them come in front of the judge—so help me, I'm not making this up—clutching a Bible in one hand and a small American flag in the other. If sufficient time had elapsed between arraignment and sentencing, it was not unusual to see the defendant accompanied to the bench by his visibly pregnant wife. Now, understand, I'm not saying that the attorney encouraged impregnation. Still, you must admit, the timing was a little coincidental.

One such example happened on arraignment day in the courtroom of Judge Lorna Jean Henderson. I was sitting right beside Judge Henderson, in the witness chair, which afforded me a panoramic view of the spectators. Seated on the side of the courtroom, where the attorneys usually gathered, was one of the best-looking young women I have ever seen. In addition to a perfect face and cute figure, she was wearing in her short blond hair a blond fall (for you guys, that's like a long ponytail). She had on a very short red dress and platform heels, which she was having to turn sideways against the floor so that people could not look up her dress. Of course, I would never have done such a thing!

After a long morning of taking pleas, this girl – who, by the way, I later found out was an exotic dancer – had not yet been called. Judge Henderson declared a lunch break of ninety minutes, and when court reconvened, I could not believe my eyes. The dancer was back, but this time, her attire would have made a Baptist preacher proud. Gone was the blond fall, which left just short hair that made her look like a cute little pixie. The minidress had been replaced by a calf-length brown jumper, under which she wore a white turtleneck sweater. Her sensible shoes may have had, at the most, a two-inch heel.

After court, I caught up with her attorney, Sissy dePriest. I knew Sissy pretty well, so I could say what I did to her, "Bitch!" She looked genuinely shocked and replied, "What did I do?" I said, "You know damn well what you did! You took that little trollop out at lunch and transformed her into Mary Poppins." Sissy laughed and swore that she had had no hand in the girl's wardrobe redo, but I knew better.

Unquestionably my worst courtroom moment happened in the mid-1970s. Among my many other clients was a probationer by the name of Roger Guest. Roger was on probation for his first felony conviction, but he had a long misdemeanor record reaching back several years and was a regular "customer" of the local police department. Roger was a big guy with a ruddy complexion and black hair who bore a slight resemblance to Johnny Cash. Back when drug use in our area was pretty much confined to marijuana, Roger was a pill popper. He would load up on pills—I don't think the type mattered much to him, as long as they made him high—and wash them down with alcohol, after which he usually became combative.

Roger had a very petite wife named Frannie, who was a frequent recipient of his drug-fueled anger. On one occasion, Frannie came to my office to report that Roger had beat her up. And boy, had he! I have seen people beaten to death who looked better than she did. As I was putting on my pistol and handcuffs preparatory to going to look for and arrest Roger, Frannie said, "Now, Mr. Melton, I've put me a padlock on the front door to my house, and if Roger comes back in, I'm a'gonna kill him!" I just said the first thing that came to my mind, "Frannie, that would probably be a service to humanity."

Well, that night, Roger *did* come through Frannie's door—literally! Finding the door padlocked, he proceeded to kick it in. When the police arrived, they found the padlock still locked. It and the hasp were attached to the door frame. Unfortunately, they also found Roger on the floor, dead as a hammer. Frannie was waiting for him when he came through the door. She took a nine-shot .22 caliber revolver and started at his belly button, working her way up in a good straight line. I saw Roger's body at the morgue; he looked like Frosty the Snowman, with little black dots of dried blood going up his torso.

Now, in those days, it was the policy of the local police department to charge someone who killed another person with murder, regardless of whether the facts indicated self-defense. The details of these incidents were presented to the next session of the county grand jury, and clear-cut self-defense cases were generally no-billed (dismissed). Before the case could go to the grand jury, however, the defendant had to be afforded the opportunity to have a preliminary hearing. Our state did not yet have district courts to hold preliminary hearings in felony cases, so if the city police arrested you, you had your preliminary hearing in municipal court, right there with people who were contesting traffic tickets and other minor offenses.

The municipal court judge that day was Mack Pyle, a friend of mine. I happened to be present on an entirely separate matter. Judge Pyle knew Roger and Frannie well, having heard testimony in numerous domestic incidents involving them. He also knew that he would ultimately bind Frannie's murder charge over to the grand jury. Still, he was obligated to provide her with a perfunctory preliminary hearing.

After listening to the investigating police officers give testimony concerning their knowledge of the case, Judge Pyle said, "Frannie, tell me, why did you kill Roger?" Frannie testified about the beating and the night she shot Roger, then she said, "I told his probation officer I was gonna kill him, and he told me to go ahead." She turned and pointed in my direction and said, "He's settin' right over there if you want to ask him."

I don't know how many shades of white there are in the color spectrum, but I'm sure I turned the whitest. Judge Pyle looked at me and, obviously attempting to suppress a smile, shrugged his shoulders. I could only shake my head no and mutter, "Unhh uh, unhh uh."

Judge Pyle caught me in the courthouse a few days later and said, "That was pretty close to what you told Frannie, wasn't it?" When I told him what my actual words to her were, he agreed: it *was* a service to humanity.

No recounting of courthouse characters would be complete without the tale of the singing operator. Until just a few years ago, most probation and parole offices around the state were located in the courthouse of the county they served. This was a very practical situation, as contact with the courts and their judges was frequent. Unfortunately, in most courthouses, especially in the larger metropolitan areas of the state, space is now at such a premium that state agencies have had to make way for county offices. But many years ago, I was working in one of those large offices which, at that time, was located in the county courthouse.

Now, being a state agency, we had our own telephone system, independent of the courthouse lines. However, calls to county offices were routed through the courthouse operator, who was located across the street in the courthouse annex. I never knew her name, but she was a dried-up little woman, maybe sixty years old. She spent her entire day in a glass cubicle, and when I say cubicle, I mean a *real* cubicle. It had a glass ceiling and a glass door, so essentially, she was sealed inside. Well, this old gal was a real hoot, and she began a tradition of singing over the courthouse public address system on special occasions. Her two favorite times were Halloween and Christmas. On Halloween, or the working day closest to it, she would sing, in a truly wretched soprano voice: "Pumpkins are gay on Halloween day, but pumpkins glow bright on Halloween night."

How have I remembered the words over the years? Well, she wouldn't sing it just once. Oh, no. We'd hear it maybe twenty times that day. She would even take dedications ("This one is for the girls in the license office"). As the day wore on, she would begin to slur the words, and by the end of the day, she could hardly sing. We came to the conclusion that either the air was getting bad in that little cubicle, or she was sipping a little Jack with her pumpkin pie. If I remember correctly, she had a real variety of Christmas songs. Unfortunately, one of the county commissioners heard her one day and ordered her to stop her crooning. What a spoil sport! And then there was the saga of the night watchman.

In the same courthouse where I plied most of my mischief, there was a young fellow who roamed the halls by night and on weekends. He was somewhat physically disabled; he walked with a loping gait and held one arm up near his chest as though he had no use of it. I don't think he was mentally challenged, although he was clearly goofy. Sort of what we now refer to as a dork. This was just a medium-sized courthouse, and the county sheriff's office was located on the first floor, so I really doubt that a night watchman was needed. I believe that someone had prevailed upon the county commission to create a job for this guy, as he was clearly not capable of doing much.

So anyway, one Saturday, I decided to go to my office to complete some paperwork and dictation. I was speaking into my recorder when I heard the door to our suite of offices open. I assumed it must be a fellow officer who, like me, had decided to come catch up on some work. That is, until I did not hear the office door close. I stuck my head out of my office and beheld the clearly apprehensive watchman. I normally wore a suit to work; however, this was Saturday, and I was dressed in jeans and a sweatshirt. Apparently Mr. Watchman did not recognize me because he asked, "Who are you?" I replied, "I'm a burglar. Who are you?" I assumed he would catch the joke. He didn't. He fled from my presence like the devil himself was after him.

In a couple of minutes, I heard the office door open again. This time it was a deputy sheriff, Jimmy Black. He saw me and chuckled, "I guess you're the burglar?" We had a good laugh, then Jimmy left, and I got back to work. A few minutes later, I heard the door open once more. It was the watchman returning. Now that he knew I was an employee, he just wanted to sit and chew the fat. I guess he was lonely. After we had discussed various subjects for several minutes, he got this serious look on his face and said, "You know, I work nights and weekends. It's a dangerous job. I mean, who knows who I might encounter? And do you know the sheriff's office won't even issue me a pistol permit?" I leaned toward him with an understanding look and replied, "You don't mean it," all the while saying a silent prayer of thanks for whoever it was that refused to license that flake to carry a gun. God only knows what might have happened if he had had one during our first encounter.

You Can't Be Serious

When I watch police shows on television today, I am amazed, not only at the professionalism of the officers but by the tools they have at their disposal. We did not have stun guns or Tasers, and the use of pepper spray was prohibited. For that reason, control of an unruly suspect frequently involved violence, both by—and more often, *against*—the arresting officer. One thing I recall with much amusement, however, is how unsophisticated our methods were for the detection of impaired drivers.

Ask any cop, and he will tell you the answer drivers *always* give when asked how much they have had to drink: "Two beers." It's never three beers or one cocktail, but invariably two beers. There must undoubtedly be some psychological reason for this universal answer, or maybe it's just because they know that two beers won't make them register above the legal limit on a breath test. The one exception I ever saw to this response was the middle-aged man I stopped for suspicion of DUI. When I asked him how much alcohol he had consumed, he flashed me a broad, happy smile and replied, "A lot!" At any rate, we did not have available to us the standardized tests that officers have today, which are complicated and require a lot of training, so we made up our own. Most of us would request that a driver we suspected of being over the limit recite the alphabet. Now, that sounds simple enough, right? But try it when you're hammered. The response would usually run like this: "A, B, C, D…P, Q, R." Confident that he had performed satisfactorily, the suspect would then flash a self-satisfied smile. Time to take a ride to the jail for a breath test, Bubba!

Occasionally, I would stop a driver who I was fairly sure was above the limit, yet he would perform the alphabet test perfectly, if a little slowly. My response was always the same: I would look at him with my best imitation of a puzzled expression and say, "Could you do that again?" Believing that he had done something wrong, the driver would try too hard the second time and *really* screw up. By the way, every one I pulled this on did test over the legal limit, sometimes two or three times higher than legal.

The city where I worked hosted a large military base, so it was not uncommon to stop a soldier for suspicion of DUI. These guys had an extra incentive to pass the sobriety tests. Get convicted of drunk driving, and you would receive a dishonorable discharge—right then! As with most military posts, ours was home to many foreign soldiers there for specialized training. One of these, when asked to recite the alphabet, said to me, "Senor, I do not speak English very well. Can I say them in Spanish?" Now, I am not fluent in Spanish, but I do know the alphabet. About halfway through his recitation, I stopped him and said, "Senor, I speak some Spanish, and you just blew it." Boy, was he surprised! Then there was the seventeen-year-old girl I stopped. I could smell alcohol on her breath, but I felt like she was within the legal limit. Still, in order to avoid liability if I let her go and she injured someone, I wanted to be sure that she was capable of driving, so I asked her to repeat the alphabet. She paused for a minute and looked like she was about to cry. Then she said, "I'm so nervous I don't think I can say them. Can I sing them?" I always recommended to rookies to never turn their backs on anyone, but in this instance, it was either that or laugh in this kid's face. About halfway through her "song," I could tell she was sober, so I stopped her and said, "Go home, and wait until you're old enough before you drink again."

Very seldom is anyone happy about being arrested, but drunks are the world's worst. While they are trying to convince you that they are sober, they are so polite it's disgusting. But once the cuffs go on, the liquid courage starts to talk. I can't count the number of times I was cursed and/or threatened from the scene of arrest all the way to the jail. Regardless of whether they were belligerent or pleading for another chance, a drunk would talk your ears off. In order to occupy their minds—and close their mouths—I would sometimes say something like, "Tell you what, I'll give you another test, and if you pass, I'll let you go." Needless to say, they would eagerly agree. Then I would say something like, "Is Mickey Mouse a cat or a dog?" See, you caught that right away, but a person who is bad drunk will ponder it, sometimes for several minutes. Or I might say, "What's the difference between an apple and an orange?" The correct answer was "They're both red—except the orange."

Some arrestees wanted nothing to do with a subsequent test and would continue to rant and rave all the way to jail. One night, I was really fatigued, and I had a foul-mouthed drunk in my car. I decided I needed a creative way to shut him up, so I said, "You know, I was going to do something to help you out, but since you've been so nasty, I'm not." This caught his attention, and he said, "What were you gonna do?" I replied, "I'm not going to tell you now. No, sir, you've been too ugly." After a minute or so of hearing him beg, I said, "Well, okay. See, after you get booked into the jail, there's this big Mexican guard, and he's going to take you to the showers. You need to watch him because he's, um, funny, and he will try to, er, *mess* with you." This technique worked so well at shutting the prisoner up that I used it a couple more times that week. Finally, one night, I brought a prisoner to the jail, and the guard I had "warned" the prisoners about—who, by the way, was straight as an arrow—asked to see me alone. Now this guy was about six six and 280 pounds of pure muscle. I knew he could handle himself, otherwise I never would have set him up like I had. Anyway, he asked me, "Hey, man, what beat you work?" When I told him, he said, "Are all the people on your beat crazy as hell?" I affected my most innocent expression and asked, "Why, Roberto, what are you talking about?" He proceeded to tell me that the last three drunks he had escorted to the showers had turned on him and tried to punch his lights out. I could barely suppress a smile.

Drunks are almost universally combative. Sometimes they just shoot a load of verbal abuse your way, but other times they actually want to fight. I was called to a residence by the uncle of a young man who was extremely intoxicated. He had consumed a large quantity of rubbing alcohol, diluted with orange juice. If you have ever had the misfortune of tasting rubbing alcohol, you know that it is horribly bitter. How anybody could get it down without gagging was a mystery to me, but this guy had. After conferring with my sergeant via radio, it was decided that I should take this drunk to jail in protective custody. He was lying on his stomach on a sofa, apparently semiconscious, but when I attempted to handcuff him, his alertness level improved dramatically. I found myself involved in actual fisticuffs, the result of which was an offender, again semiconscious, lying on the floor. After I had secured him, with his hands cuffed behind his back, I told him to get up and walk to my car with me. He refused, so I reached behind his back, grabbed the handcuffs, pulled his arms over his head, and started dragging him to my vehicle. A nosy old woman on the second floor of this apartment building stuck her head out the window and yelled, "I want you to know I'm very unimpressed with the police department in this town!" Now visualize the scene, if you will. I had just been in a fistfight, so I was tired. While cuffing this resisting prisoner, I had been cut on the hands by the teeth of the handcuffs, so blood was running down my fingers. In addition, the fracas had left me dirty. I am a very neat person by nature, and I did not mind so much getting dirty as long as it was near the end of my shift. But I had just come on duty, and I was going to have to wear this soiled uniform for eight hours. To say the least, I was not a happy camper, so I looked back at this woman and said, "Have you ever considered moving?"

Often people with substance abuse problems will drink anything, as long as it contains alcohol. I was dispatched to a large downtown church, whose pastor informed me that he had been allowing a young homeless man to live in the church basement in exchange for performing small chores around the building and grounds. On this day, he had found the young guy in an extreme state of intoxication and wanted him removed from the premises. I made contact with the man and discovered that he was, in fact, blitzed, so I placed him in custody. In a short period of time, he had consumed three giant economy-sized bottles of mouthwash! Most mouthwashes are high in alcohol content, and in this guy's defense, I will say that he had the freshest breath I have ever smelled. Took me an hour of riding around with my windows down to get my car smelling like something besides a rolling dentist's office.

Then there are the drunks who try to intimidate you by telling you how important they are. I stopped one DUI suspect several miles from the jail, so while transporting him there for a breath test, I had to listen to a litany of his connections. By the time we arrived at the booking desk, I had just about reached the limit of my tolerance. So when he told me he was a high-ranking officer in the CIA, I gave him a withering stare and said, "Would you just shut the hell up?" Well, Mr. Super Spy turned his head sideways to me and replied, "Speak up. I have a tape recorder implanted in my head, right behind my ear." Now, that was one I had not heard before, and it was really funny, so I decided to have some sport with him. I looked at the booking officer and said, "Damn! Here's another one with a tape recorder in his head. Call the city doctor and tell him to get right down here and perform brain surgery on this guy. I hope he's not drunk this time. You know what a mess he made of the last person." Then I winked at her, partly to let her know to play along and partly because she was cute. She caught right on and played her part perfectly, "calling" an imaginary doctor and having a "conversation" with him. She hung up the phone and said, "He's on his way." By this time, Super Sleuth was almost on his knees, confessing that he was lying about the recorder and begging not to be cut open.

One thing about drunks, whether they're cooperative or otherwise: their reasoning is seriously impaired. Otherwise they'd never fall for the tests I mentioned a few paragraphs earlier. You almost hate to trick them when they're so obviously hammered. Almost. But sometimes you have to get them off the road by hook—or by crook. When I started my job as a police officer, one of my training officers was Aaron Blount, a ten-year veteran. One morning about 2:00 a.m., the city had pretty much settled down for the night, and we were checking the businesses on our beat. This is the time of day when burglars hit business establishments, as they know the businesses are closed. So we drove around behind this liquor store and discovered a pickup truck parked there. The driver was clearly unconscious, so we woke him up and got his driver's license. Now, this guy was obviously intoxicated, and he had definitely driven his truck to its present location. The only question was, Which came first, the chicken or the egg? See, even a halfway sharp lawyer could present as a defense to a DUI charge that Bubba got drunk *after* he parked his truck. With no way to prove otherwise, boom, you just lost a case. Honest cop that I was (or maybe just not smart enough to think of it), I had no idea that Aaron was about to pull a good one on this guy. He handed the driver back his license and said, "You can't sleep here. Drive on home." The man happily agreed, and we left. I started to turn right onto the street, but Aaron said, "No. Turn left, then go down the street and park under the awning of that gas station." By now, you have probably guessed what happened next. Yep, that's right: this sucker drove by, and we pulled him over and charged him with DUI. What was so funny was that as we were placing him in the patrol car, he said, "You know, I just talked to a couple of officers behind the liquor store." To which we replied, "Really?" I asked Aaron how he knew that the drunk would be going in this direction. He looked at me like I was stupid (guess I was) and said, "I looked at his home address on his license, and I knew he would have to go this way to get there."

When I began my brief tenure as a uniformed police officer, I was advised by veteran officers to expect trouble from the soldiers who were stationed at the nearby military base. What I observed, however, was that the soldiers tended to be more danger to themselves than to anyone else, including the police. Their weekend passes were rare, but when they did receive one, literally hundreds of them would descend on the town. Their plan was clear: get as drunk as possible and get laid. Now, most of us have been drunk before, and we know that too much alcohol can impair your judgment. Unfortunately, the majority of these kids were quite young, out on their own for the first time, and sorely lacking in the ways of the world. Moreover, their thinking was usually severely besotted by too much booze. So when some guy that an older and more sober observer could clearly identify as unsavory offered to take them somewhere and get them a woman, some dope, or both, they were all over it. The result, without exception, was that their "benefactor" would drive them to a housing project, where he and his homeboys would beat the crap out of them and steal their money. When the cops arrived, they would be standing there, much the worse for wear, crying and slinging snot. At times like these, it was all I could do not to ask them, "Son, really, just what the hell did you expect?" Solve the crime? Are you kidding me? Their description of their assailants was "They were black males." Oh, okay, now we've got it narrowed down to maybe fifty thousand people. Big help.

It was my observation that most of these young soldiers had been taught to obey orders without question. Accordingly, if I was having a problem enlisting the cooperation of an intoxicated one, I would get right in his face and shout, "STAND AT ATTENTION, SOLDIER!" Almost without fail, they would comply immediately. From that point on, the situation was under control. An exception to this rule occurred about two o'clock one morning. I saw two soldiers, obviously inebriated, walking down the sidewalk along a major thoroughfare near the base. The larger of the two—much larger—had a stick in his hand the size of a Louisville Slugger, and every time he passed a road sign, he teed off on it. I was maybe thirty yards away when I issued my first challenge: "Drop the stick!" Well, Bubba kept coming as if he had not heard me. Considering the distance between us, I thought that perhaps that was the case, so I raised my voice considerably: "I SAID, DROP THE STICK, SOLDIER!" Still no compliance, and now the guy had obviously seen me and was walking directly toward me with this club raised in a threatening manner. Okay, time to stop being nice. I drew my .357 revolver, pointed it at him, and said, "Drop that damn stick or I'll blow your head off!" He seemed to understand that command, as he dropped the weapon like it was a hot potato.

As I mentioned earlier, a soldier convicted of DUI automatically receives a dishonorable discharge. Some were kids who had no wish for a military career, so it was really no big deal to them. But others had many years built toward retirement and/or a substantial investment in the education that got them their rank. Why they would take such a foolish gamble I just never understood. Like the time I was heading back to my precinct to complete some reports.

As I turned a corner, I saw a car door pop up from off the roadway. Yes, I said pop *up*, sort of like the hatch on an old Mercury space capsule. Although the rest of the vehicle was not visible, it was clearly resting on its side in a ditch. I helped the driver out and discovered two things: one, he was a master sergeant, a career soldier, and two, he was blitzed. Wasted. Hammered. He knew that he was going to be discharged and would lose his pension, and he begged me to let him go. I said, "Sergeant, if I could explain what your car is doing on its side in that ditch, I'd be glad to. But I can't."

Then there was the Corvette that spun 360 degrees *directly in front of me* at an intersection. As I suspected, the driver was intoxicated. What I never would have believed was that he was a second lieutenant—*and a graduate of the US Military Academy at West Point.* His only saving grace was that with him in the car was a sober female with a driver's license. Otherwise, sorry, Charlie.

It probably won't surprise you to know that some folks get real unhappy about receiving a traffic ticket. One such person was an elderly lady who had caused a minor traffic accident by drifting into the lane of a vehicle beside her. It was clear from the debris field (pieces of car knocked or scraped off during the collision) that the impact had occurred in the other driver's lane; however, this octogenarian either could not, or would not, accept that she was guilty. After several minutes of attempting to show her that the wreck was her fault, I just gave up and said, "Well, ma'am, I'm going to have to issue you a citation charging you with changing lanes improperly." She accepted the ticket stoically, but as I turned to leave, she raised her cane (so help me) and said, "All right, young man, but I'm going to put a curse behind your ear." I was not angry, but I was amused, as I had never heard that one, so I turned back toward her and said, "Excuse me?" She repeated the threat, so I chuckled and walked back to my car. For a few days thereafter, I checked regularly behind each ear, but I never found a curse there. I guess she wasn't as proficient in voodoo as she thought.

Women seem to learn at an early age that they can sometimes sweet-talk an officer out of issuing them a citation. Late one night, I stopped an expensive German convertible, the driver of which had committed a traffic infraction. It was a warm summer night, and the vehicle's top was down. As I approached the car, I observed the driver, a blond female, take her hands off the steering wheel and reach downward. I don't tend to be terribly paranoid, so I did not think she was reaching for a weapon; however, I was curious as to just what she was doing. My curiosity was satisfied when I reached the car and looked down. She had pulled her skirt up—waaay up—so that I could not miss seeing her legs, which, I must admit, were long, tanned, and beautiful. I quickly recognized this woman as the news anchor of one of our local television stations. She had just finished the late-evening newscast and was on her way home. After securing her driver's license and informing her of the reason for the stop, I headed back to my cruiser to write her a ticket. Oh yeah, I would have been glad to let her go with a warning, but it occurred to me that I might have been set up. I thought it was possible that she was doing some undercover work to see if it was true that flashing some leg or cleavage would get you a break. In essence, I was scared *not* to write her. Before I made it to my car, I decided to go back to her vehicle. And no, it wasn't for another look at her legs. Well, that wasn't the only reason, anyway. I looked down at her and said, "By the way, ma'am, that's not going to work." Made her mad as hell, but I really felt like I had no choice.

For a male officer, arresting a woman can be a real problem. Why? Well, the majority of them would prefer not to be arrested and will express their displeasure by fighting. Now, most people don't get their panties in a wad when a police officer has to use a little force to effect an arrest—as long as the arrestee is male. But a woman, especially a small one? They can bite, kick, scratch, spit, hit you between the legs, or do whatever they think will make you turn them loose, and your response has to be very restrained, especially if you have an audience. I was dispatched around ten one night to a housing project to back up Officer Wade Gomez. Gomez was of Hispanic descent and spoke with just a slight remnant of an accent. Upon my arrival, I saw Gomez attempting manfully to arrest a wiry little woman of maybe five feet in height. She had wrapped her hands around a vertical post that was holding up the porch cover of an apartment, and

Gomez had his arms around her waist attempting to dislodge her. Wade was pulling as hard as he could, but he still couldn't break her death grip on this post. Clearly frustrated, he looked at me and said, "Goddamit, DO SOMETHING!" Now remember, we were in a housing project, and some of the residents there were not overly fond of the police. We had drawn a crowd of maybe twenty onlookers, and right now, they were mildly amused at this tug of war. I wanted to keep them that way, so I took my nightstick and gently tapped this woman on the underside of one of her wrists. Ever had a doctor test your reflexes by striking your leg just below the knee with a rubber hammer? If so, you realize there's no way you can keep your leg from moving. Same thing is true with a tap to the wrist. Her hand reflexively popped open, which was good. What was not good, however, was that just as I broke her hold on the post, Wade had given her a mighty yank. With the perpetrator now loose, she and Wade did a stumbling awkward tango backward, Wade still holding her and yelling, "AAAHHH…" Finally, gravity exerted its dominance, and Wade fell on his back, the offender landing directly atop him. We got her handcuffed and were forced to pick her up bodily and carry her to Wade's patrol car, as she refused to walk. The only casualty was Wade, who was covered in dirt. On the way to the car, he muttered, between clenched teeth, "I told you to DO something." I was laughing so hard my sides were hurting, and I replied, "Wade, I did do something. But the best part is, we're out of there, offender in hand, and the crowd loved the show."

One day I was dispatched to a mom-and-pop store in reference to a shoplifting incident. As I mentioned in another chapter, I was a training officer. As such, I frequently had a rookie, fresh out of the academy, riding with me. On this particular occasion, I had a really hyper young officer whom you will meet in another chapter, Jose Rodriguez (J.R.) Sanchez, as a partner. Upon our arrival, we discovered that the offender was a ten-year-old girl who had attempted to leave the store without paying for some candy. She was terrified, and the store owner had retrieved his candy, so I decided that the best thing to do was to take the kid home to mama and give her a lecture on the evils of stealing. Well, we arrived at the housing project where the child lived, and mama met us outside, having already heard about the major crime spree darling daughter had been on. As was typical when the police arrived in this type neighborhood, a crowd gathered just in time to see mama slap daughter hard across her face. Even though this was her child, I could not stand there and let her abuse the kid, so I grabbed her wrist. She jerked her hand away, at which point my rookie jumped on her, slammed her to the pavement, and handcuffed her. I truly believe that if the witnesses had not seen mama slap this little girl we might have had some trouble on our hands. We put mama in our car, and before we arrived at the jail, J.R. had received a remedial lesson in proper behavior when surrounded by unfriendlies.

As I said, women can be hard to handle any time, but particularly when they are under the influence of alcohol or drugs. It was about two in the morning, and I was on one of our main thoroughfares trolling for drunk drivers. See, our bars closed at that hour, and apprehending a DUI would have meant a trip to court while off duty—and twenty-five dollars in overtime pay. To say nothing of keeping the streets safer, which was my main desire, of course. Of course. So anyway, I see these two women staggering along the side of the road, one of them carrying a beer in her hand. I stopped them and discovered that they were both wasted, but they assured me that they had a motel room just up the street and were on their way there to sleep it off. So I let them go. I had driven maybe half a mile when a nagging little voice told me I might better go back and check on them. Good thing I did. While attempting to cross this busy road, one of them had fallen down—and was still lying there, with traffic whizzing by her. Her companion was standing over her, and both of them were laughing like hell. I couldn't afford to chance them being run over, so I arrested both for disorderly conduct and put them in the back of my car.

On the drive to the jail, these gals decided to come clean. They advised me that, wonder of wonders, they were both prostitutes, and they offered me sexual favors if I would let them go. When I refused that inducement, they offered me money. I informed them that they were treading perilously close to a felony charge of bribery. At that point, seemingly resigned to their fate, they settled down—or so I thought. Our patrol cars were set up with a heavy wire mesh screen between the front and back seats to protect the driver from assault by a prisoner. Without warning, one of these little trollops reared back and kicked the screen, directly behind my head, with all her might. Scared the hell out of me.

Some officers of my acquaintance took abusive prisoners too personally. Of course, it's difficult not to do when they are cursing you and making threats against you and your family. I knew a couple of coworkers who were fond of administering "screen tests" in this situation. Now, you understand that I have never done this—at least I don't *recall* ever doing it—but this is how it worked. First, you had to be sure that the prisoner was cuffed behind his back. Then, you would get your vehicle up to maybe forty-five miles per hour, sing a verse of "Hooray for Hollywood," and slam on the brakes (hey, you wouldn't want to run over that poor little doggie, would you?). With his hands secured behind him, the prisoner had no means to brace himself against impact and would thus be propelled, face-first, into the wire mesh screen separating the front and back seats. Fortunately, I never saw any serious injury result from this method of shutting a prisoner up; however, I did see one or two brought into the jail booking area wearing the imprint of a mesh screen on their faces.

Street justice was something our police department would not tolerate. I saw a couple of instances where officers allowed their anger to get the best of them and stepped over the line that separates the force needed to control a suspect from outright abuse. These officers were dealt with and are no longer members of the criminal justice community. I never abused a suspect; however, I was not above having fun on a call. Many times I was dispatched on domestic problems. Upon arrival, it was common to find at least two people very upset with each other. Sometimes, when the two "combatants" were husband and wife, they would express their desire to the investigating officer, and to each other, to be divorced. I knew that when their anger had subsided, usually within a day or two, they would kiss and make up. However, on one such occasion, I decided to have a little sport with the complainants.

Willie and Martha were mad as hell at each other when I was sent to their house. Each expressed, in angry and profanity-laced language, their desire to be divorced from the other. Through questioning, I learned that they had been married for several years, and I was fairly certain they would feel differently toward each other after a cooling-off period. I told them that they were in luck. I said that I was empowered by the state and the city to divorce them, which would save them lots of money they would normally have to spend on lawyers and court fees. This made both of them happy, so I had them place their hands on my badge, and I said something like, "By the power vested in me by this city and state, I hereby declare that your marriage is null and void and that you are forevermore divorced, one from the other. E pluribus unum, God save the queen, and amen!" Both parties expressed satisfaction that they were finally free from each other, and I left. That happened on a Friday, and I was off duty for three days. Upon my return, I was notified by radio to contact dispatch via telephone. Clearly, there was something they did not want to say on the radio, so I called. The female dispatcher asked me coyly, "Would you happen to know anything about a police officer 'divorcing' a couple on Shady Lane last Friday?" Just as vaguely, I answered, "I might." She said, "Well, they want to get remarried. Can you help them?"

Now if you thought the divorce procedure was funny, you should have been at the wedding! Willie and Martha had actually assembled family and friends to witness this momentous occasion, and I knew that only a stellar performance worthy of an Academy Award would suffice. Once again, I had them place their hands on my badge, and the ceremony began. I had a small leather-bound criminal code book, which I passed off as a Bible, and I started, "Dearly beloved, we are gathered here today in the sight of God and man to join this woman and this man in the bonds of holy matrimony." Like I said, by then I had been down the aisle more than once, so I knew the gig pretty well. Part of it, anyway. I had reached the limits of my memory, so I continued, a bit creatively: "Marriage is an institution ordained by God and dedicated to the proposition that all men are created equal and are endowed by their creator with certain inalienable rights, that among these are life, liberty, and the pursuit of happiness." Believe me when I say it was hard to keep a straight face.

Willie had never given Martha a wedding ring; however, he had, at some point, bought her a cheap little diamond ring, probably from a pawnshop. I had Martha hand me the ring, which I held aloft, and said, "The ring has no beginning and no end. It is the symbol of eternity…" etc., etc. After the ceremony, I stayed for a minute to accept the profound gratitude of the "newlyweds" and to meet their family and friends, then I checked back in service. Another tough call. Hey, it's a dirty job, but somebody has to do it.

This was not the only time I had the privilege of helping join two souls in the bonds of unholy matrimony. Oh, no. Early one morning, around two o'clock, I was dispatched to the scene of a traffic accident. Seems a prospective bridegroom had been doing a wee bit too much bachelor partying and had learned the hard way that drinking and driving just ain't real smart. He had slammed into the rear of a parked car, causing extensive damage to both vehicles, though, fortunately, no injury. His intended was on the scene, crying and slinging snot. She advised me of two relevant facts: one, she had been in the car with him and had pleaded with him to let her drive, and two, they were supposed to get married *later that very morning*! I looked in this besotted kid's eyes, and I couldn't tell from his glazed stare whether he wanted me to help him get married or whether he wanted an excuse to avoid the impending nuptials. What I did know was that the little devil seated on my shoulder was not going to be pacified until we had some fun. So I looked at the bride-to-be and said, "Well, hell, don't let him weasel out of the wedding. You go down to the jail, and in about two hours, you'll be able to post his bond, so you can go ahead and get married." Coincidentally, my stepdaughter, Jeannie, was to be married the same morning. I finished my shift about eight o'clock and proceeded directly to the office of the probate judge so I could stand up for Jeannie and her fiancé. And guess who else was there, waiting their turn to tie the knot? What really made the situation amusing was they asked me to stand up for them too. So into the judge's chambers I go with these two strangers. Since I had just been there with my stepdaughter, the judge looked a little confused until I explained the circumstances to him. I said, "Judge, if you ever want to be able to say that you have presided over a real shotgun wedding, I'll go out to my patrol car and get my riot gun." He declined my offer.

As the previous two incidents illustrate, domestic calls can be fun when everything goes well. On the other hand, they can turn deadly in an instant, which is why an officer seldom responds to one alone. On one occasion, I arrived at the dispatched address and encountered a couple I had dealt with previously. Bob and Sherry were an interracial couple, and I had once stood by to prevent any possibility of violence while she retrieved her belongings from his house. Well, apparently they had gotten back together; however, there was still trouble in paradise. It seems that Sherry, in a fit of anger, had punctured all the tires on Bob's truck with a knife, and he wanted her charged.

Having helped Sherry in the past, I assumed that she would cooperate when I attempted to arrest her. Know what happens when you assume? Mm hm, that's right. I entered the house and told Sherry that Bob wanted her arrested. I explained that the charge was a minor misdemeanor and that she would be able to post a small bond, whereupon she would be released from jail. Sherry replied, in rather graphic terms, that she had no intention of submitting to arrest, and the fight was on. Now, Sherry was almost as big as I am, and it was clear from her fighting technique that this was not her first rodeo. I was finally able to get her in a headlock, under my left arm. With my right hand, I had removed my portable radio from my belt and was attempting to contact my dispatcher to advise that, if it wasn't too much of an inconvenience for him, my backup needed to bring his ass on.

I don't know which contributed more to Sherry's success with her next move, my fumbling with my radio or the massive amount of slippery styling gel she had slathered on her hair. At any rate, she was able to turn her head to the left and bite a plug of meat out of my arm. My natural reflex was to strike her—hard—on the head with my walkie-talkie. These old Motorola radios were large and heavy. They were powered by a rechargeable battery, about the size of a pack of cigarettes, which was secured inside the radio by a removable cover. To my surprise and dismay, the impact of the walkie-talkie against Sherry's head caused this cover and the battery to separate from the instrument and fly across the room. Got any idea how useful a battery-powered radio is without the battery? That's right: none.

At about this same time, Sherry was able to extricate her greasy head from my hold. She ran a few steps, picked up a folding metal chair, and threw it at me. I ducked this missile and was temporarily okay. But not for long. I grabbed Sherry again, but between the hairdressing, which was now on her arm and my hands, and the slick blood running down my arm and into my hand, I couldn't hold her. She ran to the kitchen of the small frame dwelling, retrieved a large butcher knife, and shouted, "I'm gonna kill your ass!"

It never ceases to amaze me how fast the mind can work when it has to. In an instant, I realized that I had every excuse I needed to employ the use of deadly force. This woman had threatened my life, and she had the means in her hand to effect the threat. On the other hand, she *was* a woman, and I was in her house. I just really didn't think shooting her would endear me to my department or to the community. Now I needed a plan B, and it was right beside me: the exit door. I ran out to the porch, with Sherry right behind me, still holding that huge knife. In the interest of speed, I decided to forgo the steps and simply jump off the porch. Great idea, had I not twisted my ankle when I landed. Knowing that I couldn't get away from Sherry if she continued pursuing me, I turned toward her, drew my pistol, and said, "Sherry, if you come off that porch, I'll kill you." Sherry went back inside her house, and I hobbled to my patrol car, where I used my radio—the one that still worked—to advise my headquarters that I was injured and that I had a suspect barricaded in a residence with a weapon. Finally, that brought the cavalry! While they were en route, Sherry set her kitchen curtains ablaze, so I had to summon a fire truck.

Anyway, once backup—lots of backup—arrived, a trained negotiator talked Sherry out of the house, and I handcuffed her. A fellow officer transported her to jail, while I proceeded to the hospital emergency room for treatment. I had had dealings with this doctor, having brought injured prisoners to him for treatment in the past. Upon observing my wound and learning that it was from a bite, he asked me if, like was often done with animals suspected of having rabies, I had cut her head off and sent it to the health department for examination. I said, "No, I was trying to *twist* it off, which is probably why she bit me." The following morning, I appeared in court to testify against Sherry, and she had the audacity to claim that, while cuffing her, I had held her head down on the hot hood of a patrol car that had raced to my aid. I smiled at the judge, held up my bandaged arm, and said, "I may be wrong, Your Honor, but it appears to me that I was the only one injured in this fracas." Although I was warned by the ER doctor that human bites frequently become infected due to the massive number of germs in a mouth, I am happy to report that this did not occur. Mostly, I suspect, because Sherry had a large dip of snuff in her mouth. Nicotine, in case you don't know, is used as an insecticide in some third-world countries, so I presume it had the same deadly effect on Sherry's germs.

A lot of the fun I had with people would not have been possible had they been a little less gullible. Take drug tests, for example. Now, I know this is shocking, but almost all probationers and parolees have a substance abuse issue. Yep, I know that's hard to believe, but it's true. Since use of illegal drugs is against the rules of both probation and parole, it was incumbent that our "clients" be tested from time to time. It would have been nice to have had a phlebotomist on the payroll to take care of this need by drawing and testing blood. Unfortunately, our budget was far too meager to support such a sophisticated arrangement, so we had to use the next best thing: urine tests. That's right: I had obtained, at great expense and effort, a master's degree so that I would be qualified to test pee. Years earlier I had considered working toward a Ph.D, but after discovering what I was required to do with a master's, I decided against it. No telling what I might have had to test with a doctorate, you know?

Here's another surprising fact: clients would try to deceive an officer by either adding an adulterant to the urine sample or, more commonly, sneaking a "clean" urine specimen they had obtained from someone else into the test receptacle. Hard to believe a convicted felon would do such a thing, right? Of course, an observant officer would usually catch the offender in the act. If ever in doubt, I would carry the sample back to the test area in my hand. Why? Well, urine that has just left a living body will be warm. If secreted on the person and poured into the cup, generally it was cold. On one such occasion, I was testing a parolee who was several bricks shy of a load. I could tell by the urine temperature that he had substituted somebody else's pee for his own, so I decided to turn the tables on him. After I tested the sample, which was actually clean, I looked at him and said, "You're positive for cocaine." His jaw fell, and before he thought, he blurted out, "There ain't no way, man. That's my mama's…uh, I mean…" The next sound he heard was the distinct click of handcuffs being affixed to his wrists.

For a period of a few years, my office was in the basement of the county courthouse. Down in the bowels of the building with me were three female officers, and when they needed to obtain a urine specimen from a male, who do you think was drafted to get it? Good guess. One day, just at quitting time, Officer Bobbie Starnes asked me to take one of her probationers to the bathroom. I was already pissed off—not at her, but at him for coming in so late and making me have to work overtime. Goes against my religion, you know? Now, Officer Starnes had advised me privately that if this subject tested positive for drug use, she wanted him arrested. On the way back from the bathroom, I carried the specimen in my hand, and it was cold as tap water. Nevertheless, I decided to go through with the charade. The drug test kits we were using at the time were cumbersome and complicated. The testing officer was required to place one drop of the urine on a slide, then mix it with one drop each of three different reagents. A small plastic tool similar to the type they give you to stir your coffee at a fast-food restaurant was used to mix this mess, then it was pushed to the beginning of a long snaking tunnel. After the mixture had made it to the test window, the examiner could read it. Does the description of the test slide sound familiar? Well, if you have ever seen a home pregnancy test kit, you know what this thing looked like. This gave me the inspiration for a little fun. When the test finished developing, I looked at this hapless probationer and said, "Well, I have good news, and I have bad news. The good news is that you tested negative for drugs. However, the bad news is that the test says you're going to have twins." Went right over his head, but not Bobbie's. She literally collapsed on the floor in convulsive laughter. After she regained her composure, I again addressed her probationer, "The reality is, I know you used someone else's urine. Now, here's the deal: we're going back to the bathroom, and I'm going to carefully watch you squeeze pee out of your dingle dangle. If it tests positive, you'll be in jail before you know what happened."

Where Do They Find These People?

Very often in police work, it becomes necessary to interact with personnel from other agencies. Most of them are intelligent and professional, but occasionally, you get to deal with some real nitwits.

I was working second shift (days) when I was dispatched to a branch bank to investigate a bomb threat they had received. Why anyone would want to phone a bomb threat to a bank escaped me, but upon my arrival, I was met by a district fire chief, who had also been dispatched. He was about to enter the bank when I said, "Uh, Chief, you might want to turn off your walkie-talkie." He gave me a puzzled look and said, "Why?" I answered. "You really don't know?" I then had to explain to him that radio frequencies are virtually the same as those used to set off dynamite blasting caps and that if there actually was a bomb inside, he could get us all killed. Well, he pooh-poohed that idea and insisted that he was going into the bank with his radio activated. I said, "Okay then. I'll be waiting across the street. *Way* across the street. Let me know if you find anything." Once he determined that I was serious and was absolutely not going to enter the building if his radio was on, he turned it off.

Bomb threats, of course, are usually hoaxes, but you can never be sure. Accordingly, all police academies with which I am familiar teach trainees that if they see something suspicious while investigating a threat, the *last* thing they want to do is touch it! Apparently, some officers missed that class, and they will pick up a suspicious package and examine it. If the package just happens to be a bomb with a pressure switch, it will be the last thing they ever do.

Such an incident occurred at our county government building. The building was eleven stories high and contained government offices, as well as several judges' offices and courtrooms. Right in the middle of the building, on the fifth floor, was the office of the county sheriff. One day, that office received a report that there was a suspicious object in the building's lobby. A deputy was dispatched to investigate, and he located the object, a battered briefcase that no one claimed. First mistake: Deputy Dummy *picked the case up*. Had there been a bomb inside with a pressure switch—*kaboom*. Adios, government building and all the employees therein. Then, he did something *really* stupid. He took the briefcase to the sheriff's office, which, remember, was *right in the center of the building*. And now, the pièce de résistance: he and the other deputies assembled *opened it*. Fortunately, the bag did not contain a bomb. However, it *did* house a tear gas canister with a trigger that was activated when the case was opened! Needless to say, the gas emptied out the sheriff's office. But that wasn't the end of it. The air-conditioning system picked up the tear gas and circulated it throughout the building—*and the whole building had to be evacuated.*

Firefighters are some of the bravest people I have ever known. Rest assured that if you ever see me enter a burning building, it will be to save someone's life; property can be replaced. Still, firefighters are not immune from making dumb mistakes. I arrived at the scene of a bad traffic accident at a major intersection. The city where I worked was home to a large military base, and a small car containing five soldiers had tried to beat a red light. They didn't make it, instead striking another vehicle broadside and becoming airborne. Four of them were thrown from their car before it landed on its top, trapping the fifth soldier inside. All five soldiers were critically injured, one of them fatally, so I had my hands full calling for a fatality investigator and rescue personnel. A fire truck arrived, and one of the firemen came running up to the crushed car with a jaws-of-life tool. His intent, of course, was to cut the top off the wrecked car and rescue the soldier inside. Just before he pressed the button to start the battery-cranked jaws tool, I stopped him and said, "Hey, man, do you see all that liquid on the road under this car?" He looked puzzled and said, "Yeah." I continued, "Well, that's gasoline, and unless I miss my guess, when you start cutting that metal car, you're gonna create a lot of sparks, which will probably ignite this fuel and cook this soldier. Now, GET A HOSE AND WASH THIS DAMN GAS AWAY, MORON!" Not criticizing, you understand—just trying to remind you that if you have to interact with emergency personnel, remember that they may not all be rocket scientists.

Some firefighters undergo intensive medical training and become paramedics. I can't say enough about the ones I knew. Their lifesaving skills were amazing. I once saw them save the life of a man who, when I first encountered him, had the front wheel of a two-ton car resting on his head. This was *after* he had been struck by the vehicle and had flown across the hood and caved in the windshield—with his head! As with police officers though, sometimes their driving skills left a little to be desired. Like the evening I was dispatched to the scene of a vehicle-pedestrian accident. A young child had been struck by a car; however, upon my arrival, I quickly ascertained that his injuries were very minor. An ambulance—ours were manned by city paramedics—had also been dispatched, and as I knelt beside the injured child, I saw it coming, much too fast. The driver locked his brakes and skidded to a stop about five feet from this child and me. I calmly stood up, looked at the child's mother, and said, "Excuse me for a minute." I walked over to the paramedic, who, by this time, had exited the ambulance and was retrieving his equipment. He had left the ambulance's front door open, so nobody at the scene saw what happened next—probably just as well. I grabbed the driver by his shirt, shoved him back against the ambulance, and said between my clenched teeth, "Let me tell you something, asshole!" And the conversation went downhill from there.

Police officers write reports out the wazoo (that's an actual anatomical term; if you didn't learn it in school, you should have paid more attention). Most such reports are informative and reasonably grammatically correct. When I was a parole officer, we had one city police officer who, instead of writing, like Joe Friday—just the facts, ma'am—liked to wax poetic in his reports. I was reading one which gave details of a murder that this detective had investigated.

He stated that he had located the murder weapon, a pistol, in some "cut zoo." Now for those of you not blessed to be from the south, the wild vine kudzu is the bane of southern roadsides. It was brought to the U.S. from Japan and introduced to the south just after the War of Northern Aggression. It was sold to our farmers as a method to control soil erosion. Huh! Yeah, it will do that, all right. In fact, left unchecked, it will literally consume trees, power poles, and abandoned buildings. One joke says that a lady was visiting the south and loved kudzu so much she asked a farmer how to cultivate it. He thought for a minute and said, "I don't rightly know, ma'am, but if it was me, I'd drop it on the ground and run like hell." It has been known to grow a foot per day. But the best part of this report was the next line. In an attempt to show that the discovery of the murder weapon had given him the impetus to continue his search for the killer, he wrote, "This sperm me on." I laughed so hard I almost wet myself.

Not surprisingly, the most professional encounters I ever had were with law enforcement officers from federal agencies. One city where I worked as a probation and parole officer also had an office of the FBI. One of their agents, a transplant from New York, was named Bill Dye. Whenever he called on the phone or introduced himself, it was always, "Bill Dye, FBI." I often thought he took the job just so he could say that, and I am absolutely sure that he would never have transferred to another agency, even for more money. Dye was an ex-cop from a major northern city. He was, to put it mildly, grizzled, and it seemed that nothing ever excited him.

One day Dye called me at work. He gave his usual gravel-voiced greeting: "Melton? Bill Dye, FBI." Now, Dye and I knew each other fairly well, so I could banter with him. I replied, "What the hell do you want this time, Bill?" He said, "I hear you're looking for Ronald Rice Richardson." Richardson was a parolee who had not reported for several months. I had submitted a report of parole violation against him, and the parole board had declared him delinquent and ordered him arrested. I confirmed that I was, indeed, seeking Richardson with the intent of arresting him. Dye's reply was one word: "Don't." I thought maybe Dye needed Richardson left free because he was acting as an informant or something, so I asked, "Why not?" Dye, a man of few but profound words, replied, "He'll kill you!" This was startling news, but I said, "Oh, okay. Works for me. I will *definitely* discontinue my efforts. But what makes him more dangerous than any of our other fugitives?" Dye then proceeded to tell me that Richardson was one of three members of a particularly violent splinter group of the Black Panthers and that the three of them had murdered a grocery store manager a couple of nights before. I remembered that case, so I took Dye's advice. That conversation happened on a Wednesday.

When I awoke the following Saturday, I turned on a local radio station, only to hear about a chaotic situation happening downtown. It seems that three men dressed in white martial arts uniforms had murdered a retired police officer while he was directing traffic for a local department store. They then walked farther up the street and slashed an innocent bystander across the face with a machete. About this time, the chief of detectives from the local police department, who happened to be downtown, saw what was going down. He took his five-shot .38 caliber revolver and fired at the suspects, not striking them. He then notified police headquarters what was taking place. By this time, the assailants had jumped into their car and were fleeing the scene. A police officer in an unmarked vehicle saw them and rammed their car head-on, disabling it. The suspects then abandoned their car and ran into a nearby radio studio, where they barricaded themselves and began broadcasting over the radio for sympathizers to come downtown and join their self-styled revolution. By this time, a number of police officers had converged on the scene and were exchanging gunfire with the suspects.

As soon as I heard what was happening, I knew that this was the trio Bill Dye had told me about and that one of them was my fugitive parolee. I strapped on my .357 magnum revolver and headed for police headquarters. By the time I arrived, the local police had succeeded in apprehending the three suspects and had them sequestered in separate interrogation rooms. The building was swarming with law enforcement officers of every stripe, some from agencies miles away. Word was passed that a local restaurant had brought food for the officers. Allen Ensley, a police detective of my acquaintance, walked up to me and handed me his riot shotgun, saying he was going down to the basement for some food. Now, you have to visualize this picture to appreciate what happened next: I've got a very large pistol on my right hip, and I was cradling a short-barreled shotgun on my left, like Clyde Barrow. Bill Dye saw me, walked over, and said, "Melton, this Richardson asshole won't give us his true name. Do you think you can identify him?" I responded, "Bill, I really don't know. You know, I have a slew of parolees, and I haven't seen Richardson in more than a year. Plus, you say he has shaved his head. But if you think it'll help, I'll try."

I followed Dye toward the interrogation room where they were holding Richardson. As I got close, I could hear him responding to an obvious question about his identity. "My name is Maluki Shantazz. That is the only name I have ever had." He sounded very calm and composed. It was obvious that he and his compatriots had discussed how to comport themselves if captured. Suddenly I turned the corner and faced him. In truth, I really could not have identified him. He took one quick look at me and my arsenal, and his eyes widened noticeably. I figured, what the hell, I had nothing to lose, so I said, "What's your name, dude?" His voice went up about three octaves, and he almost shouted, "RONALD RICE RICHARDSON." I knew I was about to crack up, so I turned and quickly made my way to the hallway. I was followed by Bill Dye, who was muttering, over and over, "Goddamn…goddamn. Best minds in the FBI, and a damned parole officer…goddamn, goddamn…" When I finally regained my composure, I said, "Look, Bill, he wasn't talking to me. He was talking to Messrs. Remington and Smith and Wesson."

Fun with Rookies

Rookies are a never-ending source of amusement—and sometimes amazement—to veteran police officers. Because of my prior experience, I caught on to street police work fairly quickly and was designated a training officer. This meant that out of each academy class, I would be assigned one rookie to field train. All rookies graduate from the police academy full of piss and vinegar, and the job of the training officer is twofold: work some of that hyperactivity out of them and teach them the things they need to know to do an effective job and survive.

One of the best rookies who ever rode with me was a tall slim guy named Lawrence Carson. Larry, as we called him, was a world-class sprinter and frequently competed in the International Police Olympics. My running, on the contrary, would make a tortoise look fast. About eleven o'clock one night, Larry and I were heading back to the south precinct to end our shift and get off duty. We were on Banyon Drive, not a quarter mile from the precinct, when I spotted a fight in the parking lot of Sammy's, a local night spot to which we had responded on many occasions. Of course, we had to stop and handle the disturbance, which meant that we would be probably an hour late getting off. This was not on my Christmas wish list, but I had no choice. We pulled up to the fight and exited our patrol car. I grabbed one of the combatants and shoved him against the car, but the other one ran into adjacent Banyon Park, with Larry in hot foot pursuit. I secured my prisoner in the back seat of my car, but I knew if I left him there and went looking for Larry on foot, the crowd would let my man out of the car. There was no curb separating Sammy's from the park, so I drove across the grass and into the park. Now, as I said, Larry was quite fleet of foot, and the chase had not lasted long. My headlights picked up the sight of the other fighter, facedown on the ground, with Larry on top of him handcuffing him. Since the situation was clearly under control, I decided to have a little fun. I pulled right up beside Larry, rolled down my window, and said, "Hey, Larry, you need any help?" I won't repeat his response, but it had something to do with a suggestion that I perform an unnatural sex act on myself.

Every rookie was required to work a month on each of our three shifts before going out on his own. This meant that after four weeks with one training officer, the rookie would be assigned to someone who worked another shift. I think Larry was grateful to leave me for somebody else, especially after the next one I pulled on him. We were dispatched to a call of a domestic disturbance. Upon arrival, we were met in the street by a man who advised us that his wife was crazy and was trying to kill him. At this time, the woman in question was standing on the porch of their residence, screaming profanities and waving a large wine bottle around. Larry and I went up on the porch and tried to talk with the lady, but she was clearly either deranged or under the influence of some mind-altering substance. I made an attempt to subdue her and place her in custody; however, she pulled away from my grasp, wine bottle in hand. She began approaching me, waving her bottle and threatening to kill me. I had backed away from her, but unfortunately, my back was now against the porch rail. It was clear that if the situation deteriorated much further, I might have to employ the use of deadly force. I drew my nightstick and struck her twice, but she was so wired that the blows had no effect. Just then, I saw her feet leave the floor of the porch. Larry, who was maybe half her weight, had picked her up, kicking and screaming. He turned sideways and said, "What should I do with her?" I have almost always been able to find a spark of humor in even the worst situations, so I replied, "Sounds like a personal problem to me, rookie. However, if I were you, I'd chunk her down on the floor, face-first, so we can cuff her." Which was what he did.

You've always heard that payback is hell, right? Well, believe it. Larry got me really good before leaving my benevolent tutelage. We were dispatched to a certain area to investigate the report of a man walking down the street with the handle of a pistol protruding from the waistband of his shorts. Since the caller had provided an excellent description of the suspect, we were able to identify him as soon as we saw him. We were approaching him from the rear, and he never heard us coming. I jumped out of my car, slammed the offender against the hood, and cuffed him. While I was so engaged, Larry was pointing his service revolver at the man's head. As soon as we had the guy secured, I asked, "Where's the pistol?" Now, from this gentleman's demeanor, it was clear that he was, um, let's say, a little light in the loafers. He answered, "It's not a pistol. It's an ice pick." I replied, "I stand corrected. Where's the ice pick?" He got this mischievous smile on his face and said, "It's in the front of my shorts." Well, this was obviously a job for—Super Rookie! I looked at Larry and said, "Get the ice pick, rookie." Larry looked right back and said, "I'm the one holding the gun on him. *You* get the ice pick." There was nothing else to do, so I reached into his shorts and recovered a lady's sequined evening bag containing the weapon. Unfortunately, during the retrieval process, the back of my hand inadvertently brushed against the offender's, er, private parts. Larry, of course, ragged me all the way to the jail. "Why you holding your arm out the window? Something wrong with your hand?" Finally having suffered all this bonhomie I could endure, I replied, "Rookie, it might behoove you to remember that I have to submit an evaluation of your performance. And right now, bro, it ain't looking good." I don't know how long I scrubbed that hand, but I believe I succeeded in removing all the skin down to the meat and wasn't far from the bone.

Jose Rodriguez Sanchez was, like me, late getting into the street patrol end of the law enforcement business. He was not especially fond of his first two names, so he asked to be called J.R. J.R. was about thirty, having spent eleven years in the Army before deciding that he did not want to make a career of military service. J.R. was aggressive—way too aggressive—and he had a very short fuse. About three o'clock one morning, we were on routine patrol when we were flagged down by a pedestrian. This woman identified herself as the manager of a nearby oriental restaurant. She said that an interracial couple eating there was being harassed by a bunch of drunks from a nearby table. I told her we would be right in. I parked my patrol car and notified headquarters by radio of our location and type of call; then, I noticed that my rookie was gone! I saw that he had left his nightstick and walkie-talkie in the car, and I thought, nah, no way he went in that restaurant to confront a bunch of drunks with no backup and no radio. But I'll be damned if he hadn't! As I entered the restaurant, my first sight was of J.R. standing nose to belly button with a guy who looked like he could be a professional football player. To make matters worse, there were about six others at the table—all larger than him! J.R. was being very demanding, insisting that this guy step outside with him. The fellow was not resisting but was just asking, very politely, what the problem was. Frankly, if there was a problem at all, it was being exacerbated by J.R.'s demeanor and abusive language. I told J.R. to go talk to the manager and the inter-racial couple and see if they wanted to take any action against their harassers. They responded that all they wanted to do was to enjoy their meal in peace. I then said to all the guys at the table, "Look, I know you folks have had a lot to drink, which is okay. I also know you don't approve of this mixed couple, but hey, that's really not your concern. They don't want to prosecute you, and we don't want to get involved either. So if we leave, can I count on you guys to leave them alone and behave yourselves?" They were very apologetic and polite, and we left, none the worse for wear.

I must admit, though, that there were times when J.R.'s exper-tise was put to good use. My beat went right to the edge of a huge military base, and there were always prostitutes, both male and female, working the main drag (sorry, I just couldn't resist). Many of the male prostitutes were transvestites, and some of them would fool me when I saw them, so I know they must have looked convincing to young drunk soldiers. About one thirty one morning, J.R. and I were bored out of our skulls. I said, "Let's go check Banyon Park." Now, all the parks were closed after dark, and no one was supposed to be there. I switched off my headlights so as not to alert anybody we might find, and we were easing through the park when we saw a small car parked in the grass, windows completely fogged up. I looked at J.R. and said, "Guess I don't have to tell you what's going on in that car, do I?" We exited our vehicle and walked very quietly up to the car. Inside we found one young female and three boxheads. This was a term we used to describe GIs because of the way their haircuts made their heads look. These guys had clearly been kissing and fondling this girl, and while they were all dressed, it was obvious that they planned to have sex with her. We got them out of their car, and I said to J.R., "Take this girl over there and complete a field interview card on her. I'm going to throw the fear of God into these little soldiers, then we'll cut them loose." I was chewing out the boxheads when J.R. came up and said, "I need to see you alone for a minute." We walked a short distance away, and he said, "You know that girl? Well…she ain't no girl!" I know my mouth fell open a foot. I said, "You're kidding." He assured me that she was, indeed, a he. I walked back and told these soldier boys what they had been loving on. Have you ever seen an infant projectile vomit? Puke shot out of the first soldier's mouth with so much force I had to back away to keep from being sprayed. The second boy sank down on his knees in a swoon. But the third one was the funniest. He began walking in very tight circles, alternately wiping his mouth on the back of his hand, spitting on the ground, and muttering, "Is not…is not." I assured him and the others that they had had the misfortune to encounter a male prostitute. But I wasn't through. I said, "I could arrest you guys, but I think that, instead, I'm going to turn you over to your company commander and explain to him that you prefer boys over girls." After a few minutes listening to them beg to just be arrested, I decided that they had suffered enough, so I let them go.

As I said, J.R. had spent eleven years in the Army before becoming a cop, and some of his skills were truly amazing. I mentioned earlier that there were always prostitutes trolling the streets near our military base. Some were women, but as with the "girl" in the previous story, some were men dressed as women. J.R. could spot one of these transvestites in pitch-black dark at fifty yards. Never ceased to amaze me. He'd point to one that I could barely even see and say, "That's a guy." Now, you have to understand that some of these men were skilled with their attire and their makeup and really looked like females. Often I would challenge J.R., assuring him that the person he had identified as male was actually a girl. To settle the bet, I'd pull my patrol car up to her, call her over, and say, "What's your name?" The answer, in a poor attempt at a falsetto, would come back "Frederick" or something similar. See, these female impersonators had learned that they could not be arrested for dressing as a woman. Concealing their identity, however, was a criminal offense. I never did figure how J.R. became so adept at this identification ability of his. Then again, that may have been one of those things I really didn't want to know.

There was one rookie in my squad who could be counted on to screw up, usually in a major way, at least once a week. One night, several units were sent to investigate a burglar alarm call at a church. This church's alarm stayed in a constant state of disrepair and would go off if the wind rattled one of the building's doors (literally). Still, each report had to be investigated. To make matters worse, this was a huge structure, covering a whole city block, and it must have contained five hundred small rooms utilized by Sunday school classes. Of course, each of these cubbyholes had to be individually checked for the intruders that we knew weren't there. This particular time, I stationed two officers outside, one at the northwest corner of the church, the other at the southeast corner, so that each had a view of two sides of the building in case we flushed any burglars. I took two other officers, and we went inside. We had been searching the building for maybe five minutes when Seth Parnell, the troublemaking rookie, hailed me on my walkie-talkie, "Hey, Melton, the dog man's out here. Want me to have him turn his dogs loose in the church?" Now, the dog man was an entrepreneur. He had an old pickup pulling a long flat-bed trailer on which were maybe ten crates filled with the meanest curs you should ever hope to encounter. I think he fed them gunpowder to keep them pissed off. What he would do, for a fee, was to turn one or more of these mongrels loose in a fenced business enclosure—some of which were actually scrapyards—to deter prowlers and thieves. They were true junkyard dogs.

It took me a few seconds to frame a reply to Parnell that did not begin with "Are you freakin' nuts?" I said, "Seth, meet me at the front door." Some of you old-timers like me will recall a black-and-white television program that began in the late fifties. It was about a small-town sheriff with an overly excitable deputy who was always making dumb mistakes. When advising the deputy of his errors, the sheriff would speak to him in a slow, simple way, much like one might use when addressing a child or an adult of limited intelligence. I decided to affect his demeanor, so I said, "Uh, Seth, let's…uh, let's sit here on the steps for a minute." Parnell dutifully complied, and I continued. "Now…now Seth, let me get this straight. These dogs you wanted to release, they…they weren't trained police dogs, were they?" Of course, since our department had no dogs, I knew the answer to that one. Parnell replied, "Naw, you know, they were the dog man's dogs." I continued, somehow maintaining my cool, "So…so there's no way they would have known us from a bad guy, now would they?" Parnell did not reply. I think the light was finally beginning to go on in his brain. So I went on. "And…and you know, Seth, if one of them had attacked me…well, I'd a had no choice but to shoot him. Right?" Parnell swallowed hard and replied, "Well…yeah." I continued, "And you know, Seth, in…in stressful situations, even a good shot sometimes misses. And…and it would have been a shame if I had missed the dog and hit you. Right, Seth?" He nodded weakly, so I said, "Now, Seth, what I'd really like for you to do is to get in your patrol car and try to STAY THE HELL OUT OF TROUBLE until the end of your shift. Do you think you can do that?"

Parnell was not extremely well-liked in the department. He had a bad tendency to let his mouth write a check his ass couldn't cover. This would often land him in a fight, at which point he would get on the radio screaming almost unintelligibly for help. It was up to the dispatchers to try to decipher where he was, placing a lot of stress on them that could have been avoided. One day we had a frog strangler of a rainstorm. In the middle of the gully washer, I was dispatched to a major intersection on my beat to work a wreck. This intersection was huge, and working wrecks there was a two-man job: one to write the report, another to direct traffic. Now, we were all issued raingear, but in a storm like this, it clearly was going to be about as useful as teats on a boar shoat (you may need to ask your country cousin to explain that one to you). My rookie and I were going to get soaked, something I liked about as much as getting dirty.

Well, as we were en route to the call, dispatch advised us to disregard, as they needed us on a domestic call. In our place, they sent two other officers, one of whom was the nefarious Seth Parnell. By the time we reached the intersection, Parnell and the other officer were standing in the roadway looking like a couple of drowned rats. As we passed by them, I keyed my PA mike and said, "You guys okay?" Hey, I was genuinely concerned for their welfare—sort of. At any rate, Parnell looked at me, and right in front of God and everybody, he flipped me off. I was shocked. Truly shocked. That was why I laughed all the way to my call. I believe to this day that the reason he was sent to that downpour in my stead was a little retribution by dispatch.

You might logically surmise from the two previous anecdotes that I did not like Parnell. Actually, I did. I was just afraid that his behavior was going to get him killed. Sometime after I had left this agency, Parnell transferred to the motorcycle squad, and sure enough, one day he was killed in a traffic accident. That was one of those times I would have loved to have been wrong.

One thing all us veteran officers hated to do was to allow a rookie to drive the patrol car. Of course, they needed to learn. But damn! They could do some dumb things. Like the one who was driving my car when I observed a problem. This particular road had beside it some high-voltage power lines. You know the type: they're not strung on the same old brown power poles, but run along those tall posts that are painted silver. Well, on one of the poles, where the line joined a transformer, it was arcing. Sparks were falling on the ground, and it was only a matter of time before the line burned through and fell also. High-voltage current is very dangerous, and you don't even have to touch the line. The electricity can run across the ground and electrocute anybody within several feet. I picked up my radio microphone to call headquarters so that they could notify the power company. While I was doing that, my rookie parked the car—right under the power line! I could not believe it. After looking at him with my mouth open for several seconds, I said, "Rookie, do you think that maybe that line is going to burn in half?" He responded in the affirmative, so I continued, "And when it does, where is it going to fall?" The look on his face told me that he had seen the light—finally! I said, "MOVE THIS DAMN CAR, YOU IDIOT!"

It always puzzled me that a rookie could spend six weeks in a police academy, yet let him put on the uniform and he would promptly forget everything he had been taught. Like, for example, that turning on your emergency lights and siren does not give you the unconditional right of way in traffic. I know they were taught this because I attended the same academy they did. Yet every single one I trained was convinced that he could break every traffic law on the books as long as he was running code (lights and siren). The reality is that that emergency equipment activation is a request to other drivers for the right of way. Bust through a red light and cause an accident, and you will quickly discover two things: (1) both your agency and you personally can be held liable for damages, should the injured party sue, and (2) your department will be very displeased that you violated their emergency response policy, the one you learned in the academy, and will most likely respond with sanctions, to include suspension and remedial driver training—meaning you will get to drive a desk for a looong time. Besides, as I attempted to drum into their hyper heads, if you are involved in an accident, you won't get to the call, so you won't be of any help anyway.

One of my rookies learned from experience that all rules are made to be broken. We had thoroughly discussed the caution needed while responding in an emergency mode. However, one day, we were on routine patrol when another officer got on his radio and called double zero. As I mentioned in another chapter, this is radio code for "Help! Send the cavalry, I'm in deep doo." This was a very serious call, reserved for only desperate situations, and generally, everybody who heard it would activate his emergency equipment and head in bat-out-of-hell mode toward the officer in trouble. Well, on this particular occasion, we were on Saint Thomas Road, one of the main east-west traffic arteries through our town. Saint Thomas was a heavily traveled street, with three lanes going in each direction and what is often referred to as a suicide lane in the middle. This lane was available to any driver, regardless of direction of travel, who intended to turn either north or south. Drivers are frequently inattentive, and it was not uncommon to work a wreck where people going in opposite directions had pulled into this lane at the same time and had a (usually minor, due to their reduced speed prior to turning) head-on collision.

So anyway, we heard this frantic call for assistance, and the situation sounded dire. We were not too far away; however, it was Christmas season, and Saint Thomas Road was choked with holiday shoppers. Time to throw caution to the winds. I pulled into the suicide lane, dash and dome blue lights revolving, wig-wag headlights wigging (or maybe wagging, I don't know), and siren screaming. My rookie recognized the potential for mayhem, and he started pulling on his seatbelt so hard I thought he might drop a load right in my car seat. In a voice that sounded somewhat like a cat being strangled, he asked, "What happens if somebody coming toward us pulls into this lane to turn?" I find it difficult to give a serious answer to a stupid question, so I replied, "Well, I'd suggest if that happens, you keep your eyes open wide." Still tugging at his seatbelt, he asked, "Why?" I said, "You're not likely to ever see another wreck like that."

I had the fortune—good or bad, I'm not sure which—to work some pretty rough areas of town, so my rookies tended to gain a lot of experience rather quickly. Like the one who was riding with me the night we received a fight call to the Love Whisper Lounge downtown. Now, the Love Whisper was a topless bar, and as such establishments go, it was fairly high class; we were very seldom dispatched there. But on this particular evening, two rival motorcycle gangs, out for each other's blood, had met there, and all hell had broken loose. Several patrol units were dispatched to the scene; however, I was the closest, so my rookie and I arrived first. We opened the front door to the club and beheld one of the wildest scenes I have ever seen. It was like something out of a movie: chairs being thrown, guys swinging chains, just a general melee. Personally, I was none too thrilled to have to wade into the fray, but my rookie was momentarily speechless, with eyes the size of saucers. Finally he spoke, "What are we gonna do?" I said, "Well, it's like this: we're going to the center of the room. You're gonna put your little rookie ass up against mine so I'll know you're okay. You're gonna take out your nightstick and cold cock anybody that comes within striking distance." By the time the second unit arrived, we already had two on the floor, both out cold. I clobbered one, and my rookie got the other.

Death Stinks

As part of his or her training, every officer employed by our police department was required to observe an autopsy. As I mentioned earlier, I was a training officer and, as such, almost always had a rookie riding with me.

It was a slow night, so I decided that I would accompany my rookie to the autopsy. The naked body of a large man was brought into the examination room and laid faceup on a stainless steel table. The coroner informed us that this man had died in the hospital that same day, having suffered a gunshot wound to the abdomen a week before and developing a raging infection that defied efforts by hospital personnel to bring it under control. Infections that are contained within a body cavity like the abdomen result in the formation of very unpleasant odors, and when the coroner incised the corpse's gut, the smell immediately filled the room. I am not terribly fond of the odor of death and decay, but one of the rookies standing behind me, Marty Lane, was actually turning pea green. There was a sergeant present, and he grabbed Marty by the arm and said, "Breathe through your mouth, Lane." Now Marty was very fond of chewing tobacco, and he had a big plug of Red Man in his cheek at that moment. So I said to the sergeant, "If he tries breathing through his mouth, he's gonna choke to death." Marty excused himself. I don't know if he threw up or just went outside for some fresh air, but when he returned, he was okay for the rest of the procedure.

We had a very attractive female rookie named Sheila Smith, who was standing behind me peeking over my shoulder at the body. The coroner saw her and said, "Sheila, get your ass out from behind Melton." Smith's reply was "I'm not coming out until you cover it up." Well, of course, we all thought she was referring to the patient's sex organ, so the coroner draped a towel over his crotch. Sheila said, "Not that! Damn, I've seen that before." What had her spooked was that the body's eyes were wide open. Once the towel was moved to his face, she was satisfied.

One thing (of many) I have never understood about myself is why I can look at the most grisly scenes—heads cut off, brains hanging out, you name it—and not lose my appetite, at least temporarily. But smells? Wow, they can push me right over the edge. Changing a baby's poopy diaper will send me to Puke City before you can think it. One day, I received a dispatch to a building site in reference to an industrial accident. I was advised by radio that two people were injured. Upon my arrival, I immediately saw—and smelled—the first guy. It seems he had been sitting on top of a drum of concrete sealant to add weight to it while two other workers used it as a form to bend a piece of metal electrical conduit. In spite of written warnings printed on the side of the container—DANGER, FLAMMABLE, EXPLOSIVE—these guys were softening the conduit by heating it with a blowtorch! Well, you guessed it: the concrete sealant exploded, sending the hapless victim skyward, according to witnesses, like a Roman candle. When I first saw him, he was right where he had landed. All his clothing—and all his skin—had been burned off by the explosion. The sight wasn't too bad. He wasn't charred, just very white and shiny, like the belly of a fish. But the smell was, let's say, pungent. After finding the second victim, who was not burned nearly as badly, I waited until ambulances had carried both away, then I left and prepared my report (of course, the first victim died from his injuries). Upon arriving home, I discovered that my teenage stepdaughter had decided to cook for the first time in her life. She had saturated some hamburger patties with a popular steak sauce and had placed them in the oven. I took one step inside and got a whiff of the broiling meat, then I spun on my heel, ran out in the yard, and tossed my cookies. Poor Jeannie, my stepdaughter, thought she had done something wrong until I explained my reaction to her.

When I began working as a street police officer, I was advised by some of the veterans that if I had the misfortune to be sent to investigate a report of a person who had been dead for a while, I might as well toss the uniform I was wearing, as I would never be able to get the smell out of it. I thought they were pulling my leg—until it happened to me. We received a report from the family of an elderly woman that they had not been able to contact her for several days. I went to the house and had to use minimal force to gain entry. There, I discovered the woman's body. A cursory investigation of the premises revealed no indication of foul play; she had just expired naturally. It was July, and the house was sweltering, which may have contributed to her demise. What it most definitely contributed to was her decay. It was procedure in a case like this to summon an ambulance, which would transport the body to the local hospital. The coroner would respond there, confirm that the death was natural, and attempt to estimate the time—or, in this case, date—of death. The upshot was that I was in the house for about an hour. And you know what? The other officers were right. That was one of my favorite uniforms, but despite several trips to the dry cleaner's, it always retained that smell. Psychological? Perhaps. But I never could wear it again.

There's an old saw that says dead folks can't hurt you, but they can sure make you hurt yourself. One night, my hyper rookie J.R. and I were dispatched to the scene of a murder. The suspect had fled, so all we could do was secure the area with crime scene tape and wait beside the body for the arrival of investigators and ID technicians. If you have never been present when a person dies, you may not know this, but at the moment of death, many people draw a last breath. If they expire before exhaling, sometimes that air is trapped in their lungs and is not released until several minutes—occasionally several hours—after death. Well, that's exactly what happened in this case. The man's body expelled its trapped breath, which happened to pass over his vocal cords, making a low moan: "Ohhh…" My rookie jumped about three feet straight up and came down with his pistol drawn and pointed at the corpse. I grabbed his arm and said, "Dammit, J.R., he's dead. Don't shoot him again." I still wonder how we would have explained that to the investigators.

Burglar alarms are wonderful things—when they work. Trouble is, almost every one we were sent to check was a false alarm. They could, of course, be triggered by someone trying to break into the business or residence. But more often than not, they were activated by natural causes like power surges or atmospheric conditions like wind, lightning, or even rain. Around two o'clock one morning, I was dispatched to an address in an older neighborhood near downtown. At one time, this area had been high class, with grand large residences. But its time was long past, and most of the buildings had been converted to multiunit apartments or rented by businesses. If this building had a sign in front of it, I did not see it. It was off my beat, and I was only marginally familiar with the street. The owner, an elderly man, appeared and opened the door so I could check for signs of forced entry.

Now, large old homes like this one were usually built with a central hallway, giving access to rooms on either side. The first thing I noticed was that none of the rooms contained any furniture. Just then, I entered one room which contained several caskets, in front of which was a small altar. Was I spooked? Well, in a word, yes. I thought perhaps I had stumbled into some devil worship cult headquarters. My right hand went reflexively to my pistol, and I asked the owner, "What is this building used for, anyway?" Much to my relief, he advised me that it was a funeral parlor. Just about the time my heart was settling back to normal, he said, "Let's go check my workshop." And of course, I followed him.

We entered a small semi-detached building that had probably been the kitchen when the house was built. Everything therein looked normal, except for the presence of several tables, each covered by a white sheet. In a very offhanded manner, the owner pulled back one of these sheets, revealing the body of an elderly woman, and said, "Now, this here is Sister Sadie. Died last week from cancer." He recovered the good lady and drew back another sheet. "Brother Ralph. Killed yesterday in a wreck. Just terrible." Finally I said, "Sir, do you see any evidence of a burglary here?" He avowed as how he did not, so I bade him a pleasant farewell and got the dog poop out of Dodge.

You're Charged with— Possession Of Raisins?

As any police officer will tell you, the term *routine arrest* is an oxymoron. Even the most nonthreatening situation can turn to abject terror in a heartbeat. Still, if you are consumed with fear or if you can't assess a situation quickly and formulate a plan of action that is both effective and safe, you might want to find another line of work. Either you will overreact, which can cause you a world of trouble, or you will underreact, which can get you killed.

When I was a police officer, we had a female sergeant of detectives who was scared of her own shadow. Frankly, I don't know how she kept her job as a patrolman, much less got promoted to sergeant. Let the least little thing go wrong and she would get on the radio, screaming, "Double zero, double zero!" Now, for the uninitiated, double zero is radio code for "Officer in trouble, send all available units—NOW!" Any officer hearing that call will head toward the scene, lights flashing and siren blaring. The call gets your adrenaline flowing, and responding officers sometimes make serious errors in judgment, resulting in traffic accidents. Obviously, then, use of this code should be restricted to dire emergencies.

Around two one morning, I was dispatched to meet this sergeant and a male property crimes detective at a residence where they were attempting to serve a burglary warrant. This was a very small two-bedroom home occupied by an elderly female. We had obviously roused her from bed, as the bed in her room was in disarray. What caught my attention, though, was that the bed in the *other* bedroom was unmade as well. This did not seem to fit with the rest of the house, which was very tidy and clean. Apparently sensing that

I did not believe her assertion that she was alone in the house, this lady asked me to walk into the living room with her. As soon as I did, I heard the sergeant scream. I ran back to one of the bedrooms, where she was standing, wide-eyed. She pointed a trembling finger at the open closet and almost shouted, "HE'S IN THERE." Well, I looked in the closet, and all I saw was a large pile of dirty clothes. Closer examination, however, revealed that looking at me from within that pile was a pair of bloodshot eyes. I couldn't suppress a smile, as I said, "Get out of that closet! Now!" Receiving no response, I reached both hands into the clothes pile, yanked the suspect out, threw him on the bed, and handcuffed him. With sarcasm dripping from my tongue, I looked at the sergeant and said, "Is there anything else I can do for you this morning, Sergeant?"

Another classic example of overreaction occurred about one o'clock one summer morning. My hyper rookie J.R. and I were dispatched to a convenience store in reference to a theft. The store clerk reported that a man had walked out of the store with a twelve-pack of beer without paying for it. She pointed across the road to a trailer and said, "That's his car right there." Okay, no big deal. We'll just go over and arrest him, right? Well, we got to the trailer, and all the lights were on. A woman answered the door and advised us that the suspect was not there. Then, she made a serious mistake: she invited us in. As we were talking with her in the home's living room, a small boy wearing pajamas and rubbing his eyes walked up and said, "Mama, who's that man in the closet?" The woman looked at me and said, "Y'all have to leave, now." I just smiled and said, "Don't think so." About this time, she put her hands to her mouth and screamed, "MY BABY!" I looked toward the hallway, where my rookie had gone into a low crouch and drawn his pistol. He was pointing it down the hall—right at a room where an infant was sleeping on the bed! I said, "J.R., put that damn gun up!" Then I took him to the bedroom where the suspect was allegedly hiding in the closet. The closet was one of these wide, shallow affairs with two sliding doors. My parents owned a house with identical doors, so I knew that they would come off their metal guide tracks without much provocation. I walked up to the closet and said to J.R., "Watch and learn, rookie." I then kicked the right door with as much force as I could muster. The door flew off its track, hit the back of the closet, and fell out flat on the bedroom floor. "Damn," I thought then, "I had a fifty-fifty chance of getting the correct door, and I missed." But about that time, Bubba the beer bandit fell out onto the door, knocked out cold! I looked at J.R. and said, "Any questions?"

State probation and parole officer Jerry Ashton and I worked together in two separate offices. I transferred from the first location, a small town on the extreme eastern side of the state, to a large, centrally located city, and just a year or so later, Jerry transferred to the same office. Guess he just couldn't get along without me. When I started in the smaller office, I inherited a caseload composed entirely of parolees, a couple of whom had stopped reporting. I submitted violation reports to the parole board, and the clients were declared delinquent and ordered arrested. I decided to go look for one of these at his last known address. As a precaution, I took Jerry with me.

When we arrived at the small, frame house, I told Jerry to go to the left rear corner – which enabled him to see down two perpendicular sides of the house in case the client ran. And he did! He jumped out a window and fled on foot. Now, Jerry and I were both in our forties, and this guy was maybe twenty-five. Plus, he had a good lead on us, and his adrenaline was pumping overtime, so we knew that trying to run him down on foot was an exercise in futility. We jumped in our state vehicle and followed the fellow as he ran across a wide, busy highway and into the empty parking lot of a defunct business. By this time, he had used every bit of energy he had, so he stopped and threw his hands in the air. The suspect was facing away from me, so I walked up beside him, placed my pistol to his head, and said, "You move, and I'll make your birth certificate a useless piece of paper. Got it?" Jerry then handcuffed him, and we placed him in the car to transport him to jail. I'll bet he said to me at least five or six times en route to lockup, "Oh, Mr. Melton, I just *knew* you was gonna shoot me!" And each time I replied, "If you had run another step, I'd have killed you dead as a doornail." Jerry had not yet been to the police academy for training, so he was not allowed to carry a firearm. In addition, his knowledge of the law concerning the use of deadly force was limited. After we got the parolee booked into the jail, Jerry asked me, "Would you really have shot him?" I said, "Hell no, Jerry. You can't shoot a fleeing felon. But…*he* doesn't know that, and I'll bet you a ton of money he'll never run from me again. He may run from *you,* but he won't run from me because he believes I'll kill him."

Jerry and I collaborated on some very interesting arrests over the years that we worked together. Like the time we went to an apartment seeking to apprehend a delinquent female probationer. Legally, we were permitted to kick a door down in order to make an arrest. However, the parole board frowned on this practice, as they had wound up having to pay for a few doors. It was okay with them, though, if we opened an *unlocked* door in order to gain entry. Well, the door to this apartment was not secured, so in we went, weapons at the ready. We eased stealthily down a hallway to the master bedroom and discovered two adult females asleep in the same bed. I turned on the light, and they woke up. They had their hands under the covers. Now, as any experienced cop will tell you, the most important thing to watch when you are confronting someone is his hands. People can't kill you with their heads, and very few can do you in with their feet. But allow them to remove their hands from sight, and you are just inviting them to come out with a weapon. These two women were ignoring my demand to show their hands in spite of the fact that I had a pistol pointed at them. I was getting nervous—very nervous—when suddenly both of them jerked their hands out from under the sheet and began signing to each other! They were both deaf-mutes. The only thing I could think, as I reholstered my weapon, was why the hell is it always me? We looked in the other bedroom and located the probationer we had come for, hiding between the bed and a wall.

Then there was the time Jerry and I went in search of one of my wanted parolees. Again, this was an apartment, and once again, to my great surprise, the door was unlocked. Jerry was standing behind me when I discovered this. I turned to him and said, "We're going in," at which point we both drew our weapons. I like to enter a residence quickly. I have a real aversion to standing in a doorway, as it makes a perfect frame. If somebody wants to shoot you, all they have to do is aim for the middle of the door. So following my usual procedure, I started quickly through the opening; then, I stopped. Jerry could not see around me and did not expect me to stop, so he slammed into my back like a freight train. Now, mind you, I was standing right in the middle of the doorway, which, as I said, I hate to do. Jerry said, "Why the hell did you stop?" I answered very calmly (I think), "Well, you see, there's this great big damned rottweiler in here." Jerry was trying to look around me, but I'm not a small person, and I was filling the doorway.

He said, "I don't see him." I replied, "There's a very good reason you don't see him…he has his nose RIGHT IN MY CROTCH!" Always the helpful assistant, Jerry said, "Well, you could shoot him." I said, "Yeah, and what if I miss? You know, what little I have down there, I'm very fond of." He thought a second and said, "Spray him with Mace." Again I disagreed, "No way! Some of that crap is sure to get on me, and we don't know the long-term effects of mace. It may cause jungle rot." Finally, Jerry said, "Put your hand out and let him smell it." I replied, "You reach around here and put *your* damn hand out!" Then, Jerry made a very salient point. He said, "If he bites, what would you rather lose?" I put my hand out. When we eventually got in the residence, this dog walked over to one corner of the living room, where he began pacing and snorting. I came to the conclusion that he was trying to decide whether to be our friend or kill us, so I told Jerry, "I'm going down the hallway and look for the parolee, and you are going to stay here and watch that dog. If he comes up behind me and bites me, I'll swear I have no idea how you got shot."

Jerry was a very serious guy, but if there was some mischief afoot, he could be counted on to participate. One day, he and I decided to make some home visits. Periodically, we would go the residence of our "clients" to check up on their behavior. On this particular day, we had borrowed the state car assigned to the officer-in-charge, Fred Varner. We had made a couple of stops when Jerry discovered a cache of Fred's business cards. Jerry said, "If I was really mean, I'd put some of these on doors here and there. But I won't." The little devil sitting on my shoulder had been looking for some crap to get involved in, so I said, "I will." Thereafter, when we would stop at the residence of one of Jerry's clients, I would go next door and put one of Fred's business cards on the front door. Fred said he was still receiving calls from people at midnight wanting to know why he had left a card on their door. Loved it!

One of my coworkers was a sixtyish man by the name of Charles Baker. Baker had spent his whole adult life selling self-improvement courses, vacuum cleaners, and encyclopedias. He had never been a very successful salesman, and as a result, he had no retirement account. He had accepted employment as a probation and parole officer in an attempt to build a ten-year retirement. Baker was not extremely bright, nor was he very bold, and he frequently needed some of us to assist him, especially when he was making an arrest. I was the officer-in-charge, which meant that Baker would come to me with any problem he encountered. One day he appeared in my office and announced, "Uh, Glenn, I, uh, have a man in my office who needs to be arrested." Of course, I intended to help Baker, but another coworker, Dan Packer, was in my office, so I decided to have a little fun first. I said, "Well, hell, Charles. You have the same authority I do, and you make almost as much money. Go arrest him." Baker replied, "It's Vegas Vinson."

Now, Vegas Vinson was only about five six, but he was built like a fire plug, and he loved to fight with the police. In fact, the last time city police officers had attempted to arrest him was at his home, which was located in a public housing project, and Vegas had started a riot that took police two days to quell. I told Baker, "Don't mess with him, Charles. He'll kill you." With Packer watching my back, I walked to Baker's office. Vegas had his back facing the office door, so he neither saw nor heard me come up behind him. I placed my hand firmly on his shoulder and said, "Get up and catch that wall. Now!" Vinson was tough, but he was a little slow on the uptake, and before he had time to think, I had him handcuffed. Walking him down the courthouse hall to the jail elevator, I could sense that Vegas was doing a slow boil. I had not played fair because I had not given him the chance to fight. By the time we got to the jail, he was pissed to the max.

Earl Norris was the jail warden. He was a big guy, maybe six six and two hundred fifty pounds. Still, I wanted to be sure that he knew who he was dealing with, so I said, "Earl, this is Vegas Vinson. Do you know who I'm talking about?" Earl said yes, so I went back to my office on the third floor of the courthouse, which was directly under the fourth-floor jail. Pretty soon, I heard what sounded like a war going on upstairs. People shouting, steel cell doors slamming— sounded bad. In a few minutes, I received a phone call from a breath-less Earl Norris. "What kind of [puff, pant] crazy son of a bitch [gasp, wheeze] did you bring me?" I somehow managed to suppress a laugh and replied, "Why, Earl, whatever is the matter?" He said, "I'll tell you what's the matter, goddammit! It took FIVE of us to put that little shit in a cell!" In my most polite voice, I calmly replied, "Why, Earl, I don't understand that. All it took to arrest him was little old me." I won't repeat what he said in reply. Use your imagination.

If you have read this far, you have discovered that jail wardens and guards are frequently large people. This works to their advantage both physically and psychologically, as the people they have to deal with are usually not too happy about being incarcerated. You may recall from an earlier chapter that I was briefly stationed with the parole board in a very rural area in the western part of the state. As I wrote, you could stand in front of the courthouse and hear the prisoners in the jail a block away singing spirituals. This jail had the ubiquitous bars on its windows and a heavy steel-barred front door—which, I was shocked to see, was left standing wide open! Surrounding the jail and its lot was a tall fence topped by barbed wire, and the gate was secured with a heavy logging chain and a huge padlock. Entrance was gained by pressing a button beside the gate, which would summon a guard.

One day I needed to visit with one of my parolees, who was being detained at this jail on a new criminal charge. This was before we wore a pocket badge, and I was attired in a nice suit and wing-tip shoes. Knowing that I would be entering the jail, I had secured my firearm in my vehicle, which enabled me to button the jacket of my suit. I looked rather debonair, if I say so myself (and, being the author, I *do* say so). I pushed the buzzer button at the gate and was greeted by one of the largest men I have ever seen. Now, I am six one and weigh around two hundred pounds (notice I said *around*), so I am no shrimp. But this guy made me look Lilliputian. I told him who I needed to see, and in this earth-shaking basso profundo, he asked, "And who might you be?" Now, I've always thought that being big does not entitle one to be an arrogant asshole, so I replied, "I might be the FBI." Poor fellow almost hurt himself trying to get that gate unlocked. Once inside, I revealed my true identity, and I'm happy to report that he was a good sport about the deception. Otherwise, I probably would not be alive to tell the story. And besides, I didn't lie. He asked who I *might* be. Well, hell, I *might* have been Jesus.

Vegas Vinson had a younger brother named Leroy. He was not mean like Vegas, but he was crazy as a loon (another professional psychological term). One day, Charles Baker and Andy Grant appeared in my office and announced their intent to go arrest Leroy. I knew that neither of these guys would be worth teats on a boar shoat in a violent confrontation, so I volunteered to accompany them.

Vinson lived with his mother in Thompson Court, a federally funded housing project—the same one where his brother, Vegas, had instigated a two-day riot. We found and arrested Leroy without incident and were walking him to our car when he stopped suddenly at his front door and announced, in a very loud voice, "I want to know what I'm being arrested for." I looked outside, and surrounding our car were maybe twenty adults. Word had spread quickly that three men in suits were in the apartment, and this crowd was clearly watching to see what business we had with Leroy. I quietly said, "We'll discuss that with you when we get in the car." Leroy's response, still in that loud, defiant voice, was "I want to know NOW!" I realized that we were in a very precarious situation. We needed to get this arrestee in the car and haul our ashes out of Dodge. So I bent over and whispered in Leroy's ear, "Leroy, I know what you're doing. I also know that you think, with all those people watching, I won't stomp your ass. But guess what? You're wrong. Do we understand each other?" Leroy replied, "Yes sir," and began walking toward the car so fast I could barely keep up. Would I have really whipped him? Of course not. First of all, he was handcuffed, and hitting him probably would have landed me in jail. And besides, doing that would almost certainly have precipitated another riot, and we clearly did not need that. But as I said in another chapter, sometimes you just have to do what works. And a good bluff, when it does work, can be worth its weight in gold.

Poor old Charles Baker was definitely not the sharpest knife in the drawer, so naturally, he was a prime candidate to become a victim of one of my practical jokes. Dan Packer and I were standing in my office with our backs to the door. I would like to report that we were discussing ways to improve our job performance, but I'd choke on a lie that big. Fact is, we were looking out our third-floor windows, scanning the street below for good-looking women. This was a Friday, and we were scheduled for a state holiday the follow-ing Monday. Baker walked up behind us and asked, "What are you guys going to do on the Monday holiday?" Without looking around, I replied, in my most solemn and disappointed voice, "Well, you know, the governor cancelled the holiday due to the budget shortfall, so I'm gonna be here at work. I suggest you do the same." Now, Dan Packer did not like practical jokes; however, he liked Baker even less, so he joined the conspiracy with some remarks supporting what I had said. Baker gave a little laugh then turned and left my office. In our defense, I swear that Packer and I thought he realized we were joking. He didn't. I was still asleep Monday morning when my phone rang. It was my boss Dave Drollet. He said, "I came to the office to catch up on some paperwork, and you'll never guess who showed up carrying his lunch in a brown paper bag." I laughed so hard I almost wet myself.

The following day was Tuesday, which was an actual work day. Dave Drollet called me into his office, and we laughed again about Baker's gullibility. Then Drollet said, "You know, while that was a good gag, I think you should do something to make it up to poor old Charles." I agreed, so I went to Baker and said, "Charles, I feel really bad about pulling that joke on you. In fact, I feel so bad that I'd like you to go down to Mason's [a local cafeteria] today at lunch, order anything you like, and when you're through, just mention my name." He thanked me, but I started thinking that he actually believed me again, so I explained to him that I was joking. Nice guy, but dumb as a rock.

Some people are so, umm, *susceptible* that you almost hate to fool them. Almost. In the early seventies, the parole board, using available federal law enforcement education dollars, made arrangements for those of us who were interested to attend something called the Parole and Probation Institute. This was a five-week course designed specifically for us and held at a major university about a hundred miles from my duty station. Successful completion would result in the trainee being awarded nine quarter hours of credit toward a graduate degree. Now, at the time, I had no plans to obtain a master's degree, so the credit hours did not particularly interest me. But a five-week expense-paid party at a university full of coeds (hey, I was only twenty-seven, okay?)—that was right up my alley. Student housing was made available to us; however, I decided, along with a friend and fellow officer, Ben Outlaw, to rent an off-campus apartment. This was just a one-bedroom affair; however, the bedroom was furnished with two twin beds, thankfully. At the end of the bedroom was the unit's only bathroom.

Ben Outlaw was what I call a bathroom browser. Whether he was taking a bath or a potty break, he always took something with him to read. Ben preferred a bath to a shower, and he always took his at night. One night, he had gone to the bathroom for his evening soak, and I had gone to bed. I was in what I call the twilight zone, somewhere between consciousness and deep sleep, when I heard the bathroom door open. Now when Ben and I went to bed, we both placed our pistols on the room's only nightstand, which was located between the beds. Also on the nightstand was an alarm clock. Well, I reached for the clock just to check the time. But Ben thought I was reaching for my pistol, so he jumped back into the bathroom and slammed the door. He then started talking to me, "Glenn! Glenn! It's Ben. Wake up." It took me just a second to realize that he thought I was asleep and had mistakenly identified him as a burglar. This was too good to pass up, so I started answering his plaintive cries. "Come out here, you bastard. I'm gonna shoot your ass." This repartee continued for several minutes, until I decided to "wake up." To this day, Ben does not believe that I was putting him on.

Ben waited patiently for an opportunity to get me back, and one day he got it. One of our instructors was a skinny little runt named Fred Early. Fred was really small in stature, and he had some, er, unusual sexual preferences. Oh hell, forget political correctness: he was queer as a football bat. So there we were one morning standing in an open area outside our classroom, waiting for Fred to arrive. He swished by Ben and me, squeezed my arm, and said, "Morning, Big G." I looked at Ben, and I could already see the wheels turning. He was laughing too hard to speak, but I looked at him and said, "So help me, you say one word about this, and you are a dead man." Well, of course, that was just what he did. So for the final few weeks there, I was Big G.

The town where this university was located was also home to the state mental hospital. In fact, the funny farm and the university sat side by side on the town's main drag. For whatever reason, the hospital staff would allow those patients whom they deemed to be no threat to others to leave the hoochie house during daylight hours and roam through the town unattended. One morning, after we had eaten breakfast but before class started, Ben asked me to stop my car at a nearby drugstore so that he could purchase some aspirin. It was a beautiful summer day, and I didn't need anything, so I waited outside my car in the parking lot while Ben went in. A middle-aged man approached me and greeted me politely with "Good morning" to which I responded in kind. He said, "Nice day, isn't it?" I allowed as how it was a fine day indeed. Then this man got right in my face, looked around as if checking to see if anybody was watching, and lowered his voice almost to a whisper. "Nice day for killing something." I swallowed hard and began inching toward my car, inside which was my pistol, which I fully expected to need. At just this moment, Ben exited the store, and I hissed at him, "Get your ass in the car—NOW!" As we drove away, I told Ben the story. He would laugh hysterically for a few seconds then press his palms to his temples and moan, "Oww, that makes my head hurt worse." Finally I said, "Good! I hope your headache is from a brain tumor, and furthermore, I hope you choke on those damned aspirin."

Aaron Barry Roosevelt Foreman was not a very nice guy. He had served ten years in prison for shooting a man in the back with a shotgun over a property dispute, killing him. He was paroled and comported himself as a model citizen, subsequently receiving a pardon. Then, he killed his wife, again with a shotgun, and received another life sentence. After several years, Roosevelt was paroled under my supervision.

While incarcerated the second time, Roosevelt had sent a number of "greeting" cards to the judge who sentenced him, each bearing a semi-threatening message, such as "Having a wonderful time, wish you were here." By the time Roosevelt was paroled the second time, the judge had retired and had moved to a house on a large lake in another county, and he was terrified that Roosevelt would come after him. Accordingly, I told Roosevelt that he was to have no contact with this judge. About six months after he was paroled, Roosevelt informed me that he had purchased—without consulting me—a cabin on the same lake where the judge lived, not far from his house. I told Roosevelt that he could not, under any circumstances, move there. Almost immediately, Roosevelt stopped reporting. I submitted a violation report to the parole board, and he was ordered arrested. I then notified the sheriff of the county to which Roosevelt had, I assumed, moved, Joe Bob Jackson. Sheriff Jackson was familiar with Roosevelt and the judge's fear of him and assured me that his office would attempt to arrest him.

Several weeks passed, and Roosevelt was not in custody. One afternoon, fellow probation and parole officer Dan Packer and I decided that we would find Roosevelt's cabin ourselves and try to arrest him. Roosevelt's little house was a prefabricated frame dwelling of a type frequently used by wealthier people as their weekend getaway. It was located at the end of a narrow rutted dirt driveway, maybe a quarter mile long. Right at the end of the driveway, just before reaching the cabin, there was a small ridge. As soon as we crested that, we were looking straight at the house, perhaps fifty yards away. Frankly, Packer and I had not expected to find Roosevelt home, but lo and behold, there sat his car. While we discussing our options, Packer yelled, "I just saw a shotgun barrel in the window!" Now remember, Roosevelt had been known to use a shotgun—with deadly accuracy—on at least two prior occasions. In addition, I had received information from an informant that the house was full of guns. Packer jumped into the back seat of my car and stuck just his eyes and nose above the seatback. He looked like the cartoon character Ziggy. Discretion being the better part of valor and having an intense desire to live to fight another day, I slammed the car in reverse and backed down that narrow drive at warp speed.

This was the late 1970s, and cellular phones did not exist. We had no radio, so we drove to a nearby fishing camp, where I placed a call to Sheriff Jackson's office. I explained our situation to the person who answered the phone and added, "Sheriff Jackson knows this guy. He is extremely dangerous. Do NOT send me one deputy, or you will get him back in a body bag!" Apparently she got the message; about thirty minutes later, six carloads of deputy sheriffs arrived at the fishing camp. I gave them a verbal diagram of the location of the house and told them, "Roosevelt can see us as soon as we crest the small ridge in front of his house. At that point, we will be in shotgun or rifle range of a two-time murderer who definitely does not want to be captured." Accordingly, we decided to stop our vehicles below the ridge and approach the house on foot. I had a pistol and a shotgun, but Packer had only a six-shot snub-nosed revolver, which is not very effective except at close range. As we walked up the driveway, his nerves began to show. He looked at one of the deputies and said, "I've never been in a shootout." The deputy replied that neither had he. This was not comforting to Packer.

As we got approached Roosevelt's house, I became aware of something disturbing: all the way up to about a hundred yards from his house, the driveway was bordered by huge virgin pine trees large enough to provide cover for a small car. However, as we got closer, it was apparent that the area around the house had been clear-cut—and not long before. The only trees I could get behind in the event of a firefight were small enough that I could see around them on either side—without moving my head! Not good. Well, just as Roosevelt's house came into view, we saw him run out the door and disappear into the adjacent woods. Most of the deputies fanned out into the woods to look for Roosevelt; however, one of them accompanied Packer and me to the front door of Roosevelt's house, where we were met by his wife, Alice. Roosevelt was late-middle-aged, balding, portly, and dumb, so you can imagine what type of woman he had attracted. Alice was, to put it mildly, a nasty skank. She had stringy hair and just a few teeth. She was maybe five feet tall and appeared to weigh less than a hundred pounds. And she was on crutches! Not much of a threat, you say? Well, when we informed her that we were going to come in and search for weapons, which I had a legal right to do, she responded with a fusillade of profanity that would have made a sailor blush. The nicest thing she said was "You sons of bitches try to come in my house, I'll kill you all." After a brief period of attempting to negotiate with her—maybe thirty seconds—I said, "Alice, either you move your ass out of our way or I'll pick you up and move you, crutches and all." She did move, but she dog-cussed us the whole time we were in the house.

Inside the residence, we found and secured a number of firearms, which, of course, were illegal for a convicted felon to possess. I had just exited the house and picked up my shotgun when I heard one sheriff's deputy yell, "Come back here! Come quick!" He sounded a little frantic, and I assumed that he had encountered Roosevelt and needed assistance. I ran behind the house, in the direction his voice had come from, and I discovered something interesting. As I said earlier, only the trees near the house had been cut. The rest was virgin timber, and from the gradual change in height these trees made away from the house, it appeared that they were growing on a nice, easy slope. They weren't. Actually, the start of the tree line bordered what I discovered, to my dismay, was a cliff. I knew this because one minute I was running on solid ground, and the next I was treading air. I hit the ground with a thud and started rolling downhill. In my right hand, I was holding my shotgun, trying to be sure it did not discharge accidentally, and with my left, I was grasping at bushes as I rolled and rolled. These were briar bushes, and attempting to catch hold of them while tumbling was turning my hand to hamburger.

When I finally came to a stop, I was right at the feet of the deputy who had sounded the alarm that nearly got me killed. I jumped to my feet and said, "What's wrong?" He calmly replied, "Oh, nothing. I just saw some tracks and thought he might have gone this way." Now, visualize this scene, if you will. I had just rolled probably a hundred feet through rocks and briars. I was filthy, and my expensive three-piece suit looked like I had played four quarters of football in it. And my hand was raw and bleeding. For a fleeting moment, I realized that this dumbass deputy and I were all alone and out of sight of the others—and that I had a shotgun in my other hand. Tempting.

There were several cabins nearby which were used as weekend residences during the summer, and they were not occupied at this time of year. We thought maybe he was hiding in one of these, but our search proved negative. Darkness had fallen, and as we approached one of the cabins, Packer, who was behind me, turned on a flashlight. He shone it directly on my back, fully illuminating me and making me a perfect target. Ever seen the episode of *The Andy Griffith Show* where Barney accidentally fires his pistol, and Andy looks at him disgustedly until he hands over the gun? I turned to Packer, who, by now, had realized his error and extinguished the light. Still, I held out my hand, and he relinquished the flashlight with a sheepish look. Finally, one of the deputies suggested that we might be able to locate Roosevelt with tracking dogs. A call was made by the sheriff's office to a nearby state prison, and a team of dogs was dispatched. These dogs were wearing cow bells around their necks, which enabled their handler to figure out where they were when in dense cover. The dogs and their handler headed into the woods, and soon we could hear the steady ringing of their bells, occasionally interrupted by one of them baying.

Packer and I were standing near Roosevelt's house, along with the six deputies, when one of these dogs came back, apparently tracking something. He went to the edge of Roosevelt's house, which was raised off the ground on pillars of concrete block, and looked under it. Suddenly, he began barking furiously. We were all sure that he had been trailing—and had now found—a rabbit. One of the deputies grabbed the dog and put him back in a cage on the handler's truck.

We all laughed and commented on this sorry dog. Meanwhile, the poor creature sat in his cage, whimpering and looking dejected. A few hours later, the dogs having had no success locating Roosevelt, we called off the search. Packer and I were headed back to our county when we were stopped by a sheriff's deputy who told us, "They found him." I was incredulous. I said, "Where?" He replied, "He doubled back and was hiding under the house." Now understand, we had looked under the house with flashlights several times and never saw Roosevelt. But the dog did! All I could think was, poor dog. He did his job, and we would not believe him. Bet he won't ever hunt again.

On the way to jail, Packer could not resist bantering with Roosevelt, who was in his early sixties. He said, "Roosevelt, I noticed that you had tilled up a large area in front of your house for a garden, but I didn't see a tractor or a power tiller. How did you do that?" Roosevelt replied that he had done all the work by hand, and Packer, unwilling to leave well enough alone, replied, "You must be in really good shape. What's your secret for staying fit?" Roosevelt thought for a minute and said, "Well, I only drink beer. You know, beer don't have no alcohol." Now this was news to me, as I had been totally hammered on more than one occasion on beer. Must have been the hops. Then, Roosevelt added, "And I f——k a lot." I damn near wrecked the car, I was laughing so hard. I looked at Packer and said, "You just had to ask, didn't you?"

One of my first experiences with an arrest gone wrong happened in the 1970s. Dan Packer had received information that one of his parolees, a convicted murderer, was selling marijuana and, further, that he was carrying a gun. Packer and I enlisted the help of Officer Harry Best and decided to find this guy and arrest him.

Jonathan Weekly's address was in a complex which rented efficiency apartments by the week. It was built like a motel, and every few feet there was an open metal staircase giving access to the second floor. Weekly lived on the first floor, with one of these stairways located directly in front of his door. We saw his car parked in front of his apartment, so we had reason to believe he was there. We obtained a key to the apartment from the resident manager and went to the door. I stationed Packer and Best behind the stairway, which they could use for cover if Weekly shot at us. I then stood to the left side of the door, my back against the brick wall, and as quietly as I could manage, I unlocked the door and turned the knob just enough to unlatch it. What happened next would have to have been seen in order to be fully appreciated. I was in my early thirties and in good physical shape, and I made a move worthy of Bruce Lee. In one smooth and swift motion, I spun 180 degrees, placing me directly in front of the door, while simultaneously drawing my pistol and going into a low squat. Like a Bolshoi Ballet dancer, I kicked the door firmly with my right foot, and in compliance with the "script," it flew open. So far, so good. Unfortunately, this door was of the insulated metal variety, and it was very heavy. It flew back at great speed, struck the doorstop, and returned to its original position, slamming and locking in my face. Now, I was still crouching there, trying to figure what the hell went wrong, when I heard behind me what sounded like somebody with terminal emphysema gasping for air. I turned and saw my two compatriots, both of whom had collapsed on the ground in gales of mirth. "Very damn funny," I said, and they agreed. Had Weekly exited his residence at that point, he could have killed us all. I had my back turned to the door, and the other two were in no position to defend themselves. Pretty funny so far, huh? But wait. It gets better.

We finally get in the apartment. Weekly was not there, but we decided to search the place. Packer and Best were in the kitchen, and they had found a pistol holster and several very small manila envelopes, commonly used to distribute marijuana. I went to the apartment's only closet, reached way back on the top shelf, and retrieved a clear plastic bag containing about five pounds of what appeared to be a dark plant material. I walked calmly into the kitchen with the bag and said, "Look what I found." Packer went absolutely ballistic. He began jumping up and down and said, "Let's call the police!" I looked at him scornfully and replied, "This may have escaped your attention, but we *are* the police." "No, no," he said, "I mean the narcs. The vice squad." He picked up the telephone and began dialing police headquarters. I walked into the living area, my chest puffed out. I was sure that I had just located the largest stash of marijuana ever found in the city at that time, and I could just see the headline: "Parole Officer Makes Huge Drug Bust." While I was mentally rehearsing my statement to the media, Best said, "I think you had better come look at this." I walked into the kitchen, where he was standing with a handful of—*raisins*! Apparently, this parolee was making homemade wine from raisins, and that was what was in the bag. At exactly this moment, Packer slammed the telephone receiver down and announced triumphantly, "They're on the way!"

The excitement of the moment had proven too much for Packer, who excused himself and headed for the bathroom. About that time, the little devil seated on my shoulder whispered a suggestion in my ear. I looked at Best and said, "Let's go." We hurriedly got in my car and pulled across the parking lot, where we could observe what happened next. In about five minutes, two carloads of plain-clothes police officers screeched to a halt and ran into the apartment. In less than a minute, they came back out laughing like hell, accompanied by a subdued and red-faced Packer, who screamed, "OKAY, YOU BASTARDS, WHERE ARE YOU?" Neither the Three Stooges nor the Keystone Cops had anything on us that day.

I had a similar experience my first year working as a parole and probation officer. John Roy Ledford III, alias Turd, to whom I introduced you earlier in the book, requested my assistance arresting one of his delinquent parolees. We proceeded to the client's last known address, which was in an area of town with an extremely high crime rate. Our knock at the door was answered, not by Turd's parolee but by one of *my* probationers. Now, this probationer and Turd's parolee were both drug addicts and were being supervised by us because of drug offenses they had been convicted of. Needless to say, this piqued our interest. My probationer Jack said that he was at the apartment with his girlfriend and that he had no idea where Turd's parolee was. We then informed Jack of our intent to search the residence, which we did. The search took only a few minutes, as the only piece of furniture in the whole place was a ratty old bed. However, when I walked into the kitchen, my eyes lit up like a kid's on Christmas morning. There on the counter was a miniature whiskey bottle. It had been emptied of its original contents and now was about half full of a white powder. Jack said he thought this might be salt, but we suspected that it was heroin. Having watched a lot of cop shows on television, I knew that the way to be sure was to taste it, so I poured a fairly substantial amount of this unknown substance in my hand. As I was about to stick my tongue in it, two things occurred to me: first, I had no earthly idea what heroin tasted like, and second, if this really was heroin, the amount I was holding would probably kill me. Ever been in a situation where you would rather die than make an ass of yourself? I stuck my tongue in the powder, then I put the bottle back on the counter and said, "Let's go, Turd." Turd had no idea why I wanted to make such a hasty departure. Referring to the suspected heroin, he said, "Whut is it?" I replied, "Dammit, Turd, I said let's go. Now!" As he started driving back to our office, Turd again queried, "Whut wuz it?" By now, I had spit several times. I gave Turd this baleful look and replied, "It was SALT, dammit! Now drive."

As the above story indicates all too clearly, things are not always what they appear to be. Take the case of the fire chief's car.

Ray Langford was the chief of our city's fire department and a heck of a nice guy. His wife, Betsy, was a crossing guard at a local elementary school and was also well-liked. One afternoon, as Betsy was shepherding the children safely across the street from school, she saw two men drive away in her brand-new Buick Riviera. This, of course, was not a happy sight, so she immediately called the police department, and a BOLO (be on the lookout) was issued via radio. The dispatcher added that the vehicle belonged to the spouse of the fire chief, which gave us a little extra impetus to find it. The only problem was that Betsy did not know the license plate number.

Generally, vehicles are stolen by one of two types of offenders. The first are juveniles, who take the car for a joyride. Usually they are fairly easy to apprehend because they keep the vehicle on the road, showing it off and giving rides to their friends until it runs out of gas, at which time they will often abandon it. If the car is taken by a professional, on the other hand, there is only a brief window of opportunity for locating it before it winds up out of sight, usually in a chop shop, where it will be dismantled and the parts sold to unscrupulous repair facilities.

Most of the time, within an hour after a BOLO for a stolen vehicle has been broadcast, the information goes cold in an officer's memory bank. There are other calls to handle, and watching for the vehicle assumes a lower priority among the officer's powers of observation. Imagine my surprise, then, when what to my wondering eyes should appear but a new Buick Riviera heading *right toward me.* It was clear that the female (yes, female) driver did not want me to see her, as she made a hard left turn directly in front of my patrol car. Well, hell, after she did that, she might as well have had a sign on her car saying "Follow me." I radioed my location to my dispatcher and advised that I was directly behind what I thought was the stolen Buick. Problem was, I could not get a reading on the tag because shadowing the Buick closely was a black Thunderbird. It was obvious that the two vehicles were traveling together because every time I tried to move a little left in order to read the Buick's tag, the Thunderbird would also move over, intentionally blocking my view. Finally, I faked the driver out by moving left, then quickly back to the right. He fell for the move, and I was able to read the tag number and relay it to dispatch. After a pause of only seconds, the dispatcher replied, with obvious tension in his voice, "That's it! You've got it. All units hold traffic on channel two. Three oh seven [my unit number], keep me advised of your 10-20 [location]."

I was sure that other units in the area were converging on my position to provide backup when I attempted to stop these vehicles; however, the two cars were getting dangerously close to Saint Thomas Road. This was a heavily traveled east-west thoroughfare that ran right through the heart of town, and I knew that a vehicle pursuit in that kind of traffic might result in an accident with injury or death to innocent drivers. The two cars were now just a block from Saint Thomas Road, on Harriet Street. I decided that, backup or not, I had to try to stop them. I did not activate my emergency lights or siren, as I wanted my next action to come as a surprise to them, hopefully not giving them time to flee. I floored my accelerator, passing them, and when I was maybe a hundred feet ahead, I locked my brakes and turned my patrol car sideways in the narrow street, effectively blocking their path.

I immediately radioed dispatch of my location and situation. At the same instant, I heard three sirens being activated, the nearest of which sounded like it was five miles away. There was no need for responding units to maintain silence any more, and they were coming full bore. I secured the female driver of the Buick, who would later say that I pointed a gun in her face that looked like a cannon (more about that later). The driver of the Thunderbird, however, was being uncooperative. He kept reaching under his seat, and I kept ordering him to place his hands on the steering wheel, as I was afraid he might be reaching for a gun (he was, but not for the reason I thought). My final verbal communication to him was loud and very clear. I said, "Move your hands one more time, and I swear it will be the last thing you ever do!" At about this time, a whole bunch of people began arriving. Most were fellow officers, who helped me secure both prisoners, but there were also reporters from the local television stations who had been listening to the drama unfold on their scanners.

From the Thunderbird, we recovered a semiautomatic pistol right under the driver's seat, as I had thought. The female was placed in another patrol car, but I had the Thunderbird driver in mine and was transporting him to jail when I was notified by radio to take both suspects to the office of the police chief. Now, it wasn't uncommon for the chief to personally congratulate an officer who had just done something really commendable, as I assumed I had. But bring the suspects to his office? Well, that was unheard of. Clearly, something was up, but what? As soon as I arrived at headquarters, I found out.

Chief Joe Waterford was tall and lean, and he had a booming voice. During encounters with him, you had no doubt who was in charge. He said, "Melton, you did a great job out there [chest puffing time]. Unfortunately, you also busted up the best sting we have had going in a long time [oops]." He then introduced me to the two "suspects." The driver of the Buick had recently been hired as a police officer by our department, but she had not been to the academy, and none of us had ever seen her. The male was a state trooper, serving as an investigator. Turns out the Buick had actually been stolen, but it had been bought by these two "fences," and they were taking it to an impound lot when I encountered them. The trooper had actually been reaching for his gun, hoping to hide it so well that we would not find it and blow his cover. The chief and one sergeant were the only officers in our department who knew anything about the operation.

As I left the chief's office, I ran smack into the major in charge of patrol. He was standing with one of the television reporters, and he said, "There's the officer who took 'em down. You might want to talk to him." I looked at him, sadly I'm sure, and replied, "Major, there's more to this than meets the eye. You might want to have a sit-down with the chief." From officer of the month to goat (an innocent one, but still a goat) in about one hour. Oh well, like they say, stuff happens.

Epilogue

Alas, as with careers, books must come to an end, and this one has. I hope you have enjoyed reading it as much as I enjoyed writing it. Most of all, I hope that it has shown you that not all cops are humorless automatons. We have a serious job, but most of us try to inject some levity when possible. Makes the sad and dangerous parts a little more tolerable.

And now, if you will permit me one conceit, I would like to leave you with a thought I attempted to pass on to all my rookies. Laugh a little every day. It won't make your face crack, and I absolutely guarantee you'll enjoy your life more.

Then again, I might just be joking.

Ciao.

About the Author

Glenn Melton is a retired law enforcement officer. During his thirty-five-year career, he was, at different times, a police officer, a juvenile probation officer, and an adult probation and parole officer.

Glenn and his wife, Jayne, a retired warrant magistrate, live in north Alabama. They enjoy spending time with their three adult children and three grandchildren. In their spare time, they enjoy golf.

www.ingramcontent.com/pod-product-compliance
Lightning Source LLC
Chambersburg PA
CBHW051445250726
48655CB00001B/251